The German Great Escape

For My Mother, Barbara

The German Great Escape

The Story of Island Farm

Peter Phillips

seren

Seren is the book imprint of
Poetry Wales Press Ltd
Nolton Street, Bridgend, CF31 3BN
www.seren-books.com

The right of Peter Phillips to be identified
as the Author of this Work has been asserted
in accordance with the Copyright, Designs
and Patents Act, 1988

ISBN 1-85411-383-6

The publisher works with the support of the Welsh Books Council

Printed in Plantin by CPD (Wales) Ebbw Vale

CONTENTS

1. Appease or Arm?

When Prime Minister Stanley Baldwin and his coalition Cabinet met on 28 April 1936, they were to finalise plans to build what would be the largest munitions factory in Europe. It was a massive construction project that would transform a 1,200 acre green field site into an arsenal employing 40,000 people and be fully operational within four years. The location presented for approval was Bridgend, in south Wales. The decision was tangible proof of the British Government's gradual acceptance that war was becoming increasingly likely, and that Britain was ill-equipped for the eventuality. Events around the world – and particularly in Europe – cast doubt on the notion, held since 1918, that Britain and its allies had fought and won 'the war to end all wars'.

The widely held belief that the surrender terms imposed on Germany after the First World War led to Hitler's power, and that he alone was responsible for the carnage of the Second World War, is sound though far too simplistic. Six months of discussion between the victors at the Paris Conference of 1919 were dominated by the U.S. President, Woodrow Wilson, and resulted in the Treaty of Versailles. Germany was to lose thirteen per cent of its national territory, including the Baltic port of Danzig (now known as Gdansk) which created the so-called 'Polish Corridor', that separated East Prussia, the birthplace of German nationalism, from the rest of the country. All German colonies were confiscated. The German Army was to be reduced to 100,000 men and the Navy to the size of a coastal defence force. Conscription was prohibited. The heart of German industry, the Ruhr, was put under Allied control and a demilitarised zone extended into the Rhineland to serve as a buffer. In addition, German financial assets were seized and reparations of £6.6 billion (at 1919 values) were to be paid to the Allies in annual installments until 1983.

The Paris Conference also gave birth to the League of Nations, from which Germany was excluded; essentially world affairs were to be placed in the hands of responsible powers. The treaty created a divide between the 'Haves' and 'Have-Nots'. The former consisted of Britain and France, which together ruled directly or indirectly over one third of the globe, and America, with its policy of isolation.

The wild card was Russia, easily capable of being a world power, but embarking on a journey through the previously uncharted waters of Communism.

Despite utter disbelief, and anger, throughout the country at the terms of the Versailles Treaty, the German Government, guided by the Foreign Minister, Gustav Stresemann, adopted a conciliatory attitude and a policy of long-term diplomacy to gradually revise the conditions. The German economy, like those of Britain and France after the war, was decimated. However Germany had no economic oxygen to aid recovery and the result was hyperinflation and a plummeting currency. As reparation payments were calculated in Sterling it was only a matter of time before Germany was unable to pay.

French reaction, when payment defaulted, was to occupy the Ruhr coalfield on 9 January 1923. Nine months later it was obvious that this would not force a bankrupt German Treasury to recommence payments, and it was agreed that the United States should mediate. Opportunism came to the fore when the Chairman of the mediation committee, leading New York banker Charles Dawes, suggested the solution. The United States would make a series of substantial bank loans to Germany which would be used not only for compensation payments to the Allies but for industrial investment and to introduce a new currency, the Rentenmark.

With the heat taken out of the situation, over the following two years Stresemann continued his strategy, and a new treaty was signed in October 1925 between Germany, Britain, France, Belgium and Italy at Locarno. In it Germany gained admission to the League of Nations, the Allied military occupation of the Rhineland ended and inspections of the German armed forces were curtailed. However the new harmony was overturned four years later with the Wall Street Crash that caused a domino effect on all Western economies. The result of the American banking crisis was the suspension of loans to Germany, and consequently reparation payments to the Allies. The position was universally accepted: nobody was minded, or in a position, to threaten military action. The focus of government, and individuals, turned to financial survival.

In Germany unemployment soared from 1.4 million in 1928 to 6 million by 1932. The German President, Paul von Hindenburg, now without the guiding hand of Stresemann who had died in 1929, was forced, at one point, to suspend the Reichstag due to acrimonious disputes within the German parliament and increasingly violent demonstrations outside the building. These conditions were exploited by the increasingly influential right wing National Socialist Workers Party.

When Britain counted the cost of the First World War in terms of life and money, there was no public appetite for further aggression, and successive governments through the 1920s focussed on rebuilding the shattered economy. David Lloyd George, the Liberal Prime Minister, returned from Versailles in the belief that Germany had been too harshly treated and fearing that the treaty would lead to political extremism, by both left and right wing activists. His position of allowing Germany a degree of leeway as it restored itself was broadly followed by his successors, Bonar Law, Baldwin and Ramsay MacDonald. The fragile improvement in the post-war British economy hit a serious setback in 1926 with the calling of the General Strike. Four years later the stock market collapse heralded prolonged depression and rampant unemployment. By 1931 the Coalition Government was facing swathing cuts; whatever individual views were of darkening forces in Europe, the resources for rearmament remained scarce.

The totalitarian regimes of Mussolini in Italy and Stalin in Russia, began to appear as the way out of the misery of economic depression. Italy became the first of the 'Have-Nots' to attempt promotion to the premier league of imperial powers. Mussolini had come to power in 1922 with a popular public works programme as the foundation for his vision of restoring a Roman empire throughout the Mediterranean and Middle East.

Meanwhile, unhindered by arms inspection, which had been gradually declined following the Locarno Treaty, the German Chancellor, Franz von Papen, authorised an accelerated, and secret, programme of rearmament. When the World Disarmament Conference met for the first time in 1932, the German delegation walked out, refusing to return, unless they were allowed to develop their armed forces to a level commensurate with the major European powers. Already on an aggressive path, within a year Germany had a new Chancellor, Adolf Hitler.

Austrian-born Hitler had seen front line service in the War, suffering temporary blindness following a mustard gas attack in Belgium. Recognising the humiliation and anger felt by many Germans at the terms of the surrender, amid the post-war anarchy and rumour he quickly became known in Bavaria as a forceful orator, telling inflation-ravaged audiences, terrified of a Communist takeover, exactly what they wanted to hear. By July 1921 he had risen to be Chairman of the National Socialist German Worker's Party, or Nazis. Hitler proceeded to indoctrinate followers with his vision for Germany and what he considered to be the real cause for its woes, Jews.

In an attempt to preserve public order immediately after the war, and to crush possible Communist insurgency, veterans formed vigilante groups. The largest was the paramilitary *Frei Korps* (S.A.) which, in its uniform of brown shirts, became the militia of the Nazi party. In November 1923, with this new found military might, and the inflation crisis deepening, Hitler saw an opportunity. In an operation known as the Munich Putsch, Hitler and a force of 2,000 S.A. attempted to seize control of the Bavarian Government. The police put down the revolt but Hitler used the resulting trial, at which he was sentenced to five years imprisonment, as a propaganda platform to deliver his view to a wider audience.

Hitler served only eight months in prison, using the time to document his anti-Semitism and vision for Germany in a book, *Mein Kampf* (My Struggle). On his release he set about reviving the Nazi Party, structured this time along the Fuhrer principle of an absolute leader. In September 1925 Hitler's bodyguard and driver, Julius Schreck, formed an elite group from the handful of colleagues most loyal to the Fuhrer. They wore distinctive black uniforms and became known as the *Schutz Staffel* (Protection Squad) or S.S. Within a year the S.S. had grown to be an Army within an Army and was commanded by one of Hitler's most devoted followers, Heinrich Himmler.

With ambition now well beyond a localised military coup, the Nazi party set out to achieve control of the German parliament, the Reichstag, by democratic means. Hitler's mastery of mass psychology, and his almost mesmeric ability in front of mass audiences desperate for a radical solution to their problems, was augmented by the strategic planning skills of Joseph Goebbels and Hermann Goering.

In the general election of 1928 the Nazi Party won 12 seats. Goebbels took over responsibility for propaganda before the following election in 1930 where, despite gaining 107 seats, the party was not allowed to form a government. Now attracting the support of business, Hitler spoke at three massive rallies in the run-up to the presidential election of March 1932, which he lost narrowly to the incumbent Hindenburg. With the country in deepening financial crisis, governed by a weakened President with a barely workable majority, and amid growing civil unrest, the Nazi Party achieved a landslide victory in the subsequent November general election. Von Hindenburg had no alternative but to appoint Hitler as Chancellor the following January.

Hitler did not intend to govern with a constitution in which he was subservient to a higher authority. Amid rumours of Communist plotting, the Reichstag building was badly damaged by fire on 27 February 1927. Hitler demanded that von Hindenburg call a state of emergency and suspend all civil liberties. Another election was called in March and, with the S.A. and S.S. troops a threatening presence at polling booths, the Nazi Party was returned with the two-thirds majority necessary to reform the constitution.

On 23 March the Reichstag passed the Enabling Act that gave dictatorial power to Hitler's cabinet for four years. Under a policy called *Gleichschaltung*, or co-ordination, Hitler proceeded to subordinate all independent institutions to the authority of the Nazi Party. By July it was the only legal political party in Germany. When von Hindenburg died on 2 August 1934, Hitler abolished the office of President. The Third Reich was born.

The Fuhrer's attention was also directed inward. On 30 June 1934 – 'the Night of the Long Knives' – Himmler's S.S. executed over 100 dissident members of the Nazi Party including the head of the S.A. Now in complete control of both party and country, Hitler began to reveal his longer-term aims. Laws were passed withdrawing many basic human rights from Jews. A secret police force, the Gestapo, was formed. The Fuhrer spoke increasingly about *lebensraum* (living space) for the German people. To accommodate their needs he looked eastwards at the vast Polish and Russian farmlands. In the short term he was looking at political unification with Austria and German parts of Czechoslovakia.

The first Nazi move outside of German borders was a stunning piece of diplomacy. Germany pressed for the people of the coalmining Saar region, under the control of the League of Nations since 1919, to be given the right to choose their Government. In a referendum they overwhelmingly voted for a return to German rule.

One of Hitler's first actions as Chancellor had been to withdraw Germany simultaneously from the League of Nations, and the much-trumpeted World Disarmament Conference. Unrestrained, Hitler announced to the delight of his former electorate that the Army was to be increased to 240,000. With the introduction of conscription it grew to 550,000 in less than three years. Similar plans to increase the navy were announced, as was, for the first time, the formation of a German air force, banned under the Treaty of Versailles.

The first major act of aggression since the end of the 1914-18 war took place in September 1931 when Japan, another 'Have-Not', invaded the Chinese province of Manchuria and set up a puppet state. Two years later Japan also left the League of Nations. In September 1935, Mussolini's Italian troops invaded Abyssinia (now known as Ethiopia). Hitler's first act of foreign aggression occurred in March 1936 when German troops reclaimed, unopposed, the Rhineland. Not only was the diplomatically driven peace at an end, the League of Nations was redundant.

With hindsight of the horror that was to unfold over the following ten years, it is hard to believe that the reaction of the British Government, and much of the public, to Hitler's rise to power and to world events, was so apathetic. With no appetite, or financial resources to fight a major war, great public faith had been placed in the League of Nations. To the man on the Clapham Omnibus, and to many political and business circles, the rise of fascism was not perceived as so great a threat as that posed by Russian Communism. Anthony Eden reported the comments of his taxi driver who, lecturing on the Rhineland crisis, told the Foreign Secretary that Hitler was merely 'going into his own back-yard'. Voices of concern, notably that of Winston Churchill, from his Parliamentary backbench, were in a small minority.

The stance of the British Government during that second half of the 1930s is often termed 'appeasement' but this tag is probably not a fair, or accurate, description. An important development resulting from the Great War was placing of more credence in diplomacy. Most of the British media, including the B.B.C., which then had much more freedom to take an editorial position, supported this approach. In Germany Hitler's PR machine presented him as a peacemaker, especially in relations with Britain.

Many modern historians subscribe to the theory that Hitler's original strategy included working closely with the British Empire, which he admired. Certainly, when Hitler became Chancellor the British Government made high profile efforts towards a positive relationship with him. In June 1935 an Anglo-German naval agreement was made which reflected Hitler's ability in public relations and negotiation. It was accepted in Britain that naval rivalry between the two countries had been a major cause of the previous war, and a common sense approach from the new German leader was consequently welcomed. Hitler, meanwhile, used the agreement as proof that the British government now recognised the German right to rearm. He had conceded little, as even with a committed programme, it would take several years for the German Navy to reach the limits agreed.

The coalition National Government formed after the 1935 general election in Britain was not as myopic to the unfolding events as it has been accused. It commissioned a secret report into the condition of the British armed forces and their requirements. The findings were disturbing. Naval vessels were outdated and the fleet was dangerously overstretched. The Army was now only slightly larger than that of Germany, and 75% of troops were posted outside of Europe. German investment in armament outstripped British by 300%. In aircraft production, the key area in modern war according to military planners, German output in the previous two years had exceeded Britain's by 5,951 to 1,880.

The mood of the Cabinet Meeting on 28 April 1936 was sombre. No one could argue that Britain was pitifully unprepared for war. An air of realism following the Italian invasion of Abyssinia and, more importantly, the German occupation of the Rhineland made even the staunchest supporters of appeasement accept that war was increasingly probable. The fundamental problem facing the Government was that it had been elected on a manifesto of social investment and the public were far from convinced of the dangers looming in Europe and beyond.

The cabinet reached an uneasy compromise. A four-year investment plan to re-arm was to start immediately, raising expenditure from £185 million in the current year to £719 million in 1939; figures grudgingly accepted by the Treasury. Military and Government advice was in tandem: continue with diplomacy for as long as possible, if only to delay the start of a war until 1940.

Each branch of the armed forces began fighting over its share of the new budget. However the common denominator to all military needs was ammunition. Expanding the historic but confined and antiquated Woolwich Arsenal – now in easy range of European-launched bombers – was not an option. A new, state-of-the-art, munitions factory was to be built and Bridgend, a small town between Cardiff and Swansea, was chosen as the location.

2. THE BIGGEST FACTORY EVER BUILT

History can be unkind to British Prime Ministers. Supporters of Neville Chamberlain would never argue for his greatness, but his image as a naive idealist, dressed in outdated winged collars and frock coats, impotently trying to appease Hitler as Europe moved towards war, is unfair.

Stanley Baldwin surprised press and Parliament when he unexpectedly stood down as Prime Minister in May 1937 and Chamberlain, who had been Chancellor of the Exchequer for the previous six years, was the natural successor. Born in 1868, a successful businessman, he entered Parliament as the Conservative M.P. for Birmingham Ladywood in 1918. By 1924 he had reached the Cabinet. His assessment of the situation in Europe, and the prospects for Britain, when he became Prime Minister, was pessimistic. The ambition of Germany's new leader was increasingly apparent and Britain was not in a position to enter a major conflict.

While the British Government was finalising plans for massive rearmament, Hitler was still seeking an Anglo-German alliance. During the summer of 1936, the German Ambassador, Joachim von Ribbentrop, was attending a series of diplomatic meetings. His son being refused entry to Eton may have coloured Ribbentrop's anti-British views, but he accurately reported to Berlin that Britain was not prepared to allow Germany a free hand in Europe in return for the Fuhrer's guarantee that he had no intentions on Britain.

Hitler's reaction was to announce to the Nazi hierarchy a plan for the total domination of mainland Europe. His Memorandum of August 1936 outlined two 'tasks': first, that the German Army be combat-ready within four years; secondly, that the economy be capable of war in the same period. Implementation was to be overseen by Hermann Goering, now Hitler's chief military strategist. Britain and Germany were now working to the same timetable for rearmament.

Whether Chamberlain knew of Hitler's plan is still not public knowledge, but he was aware of an agreement signed in October 1936 between Germany and Italy, in which Europe's two fascist dictators promised closer collaboration. Presented to the world as a 'treaty of friendship' it joined two like-minded regimes and provided a platform for their joint aspirations. The following month Germany entered into the Anti-Comintern Pact with Japan. Italy would join within a year. An axis of power had been established that would last until 1945.

Chamberlain was not an aggressor and believed passionately in the strategy of diplomacy over war. He was not, however, a pacifist; instead, he was a realist. Knowing Britain would not be prepared for war until 1940, at the earliest he decided on a common sense course. Britain would continue to negotiate in good faith with Hitler, making concessions and allowances if necessary, in the hope that conflict could somehow be avoided at least until Britain was geared up for a full-scale war. If Chamberlain's outward policy of appeasement worked it would be against the odds, but in any event it would buy valuable time for the rearmament programme. Even with hindsight it was the right strategy. However, Chamberlain made three critical mistakes.

Hitler had invited Lord Halifax, the British Foreign Secretary and a close advisor to Chamberlain, to Berlin for informal talks. Halifax used the occasion to outline his Government's position, which was favourable to a peaceful settlement by Germany of its post-Versailles grievances in respect of Austria and Czechoslovakia. Unknown to Hitler, Chamberlain would also have been prepared to allow a peaceful German return to Danzig and the contentious Polish Corridor. Hitler stressed to Halifax that all Germany wanted was to have a 'free hand' in resolving its problems in Eastern Europe. Nothing tangible was agreed, but both sides declared the talks a great success.

However, on 5 November 1937, two weeks before the visit of Halifax's, Hitler had outlined his Memorandum to a carefully chosen group of military advisors. Austria and Czechoslovakia were to be seized, by force if necessary. Hitler's view was that this would probably provoke Britain and France to declare war, but it was a risk that he was prepared to take. To ensure support for his plans, he had removed two leading Army moderates and appointed himself as Chief of the armed forces. This was an extremely dangerous strategy as Hitler was far short of securing the confidence of his Generals, many of whom had not recovered from the shock of defeat in the Great War. The consensus of opinion amongst senior German military men was that Hitler was too ambitious, and with the country still not prepared for war, nothing should be done to begin one prematurely.

The final descent to war began in January 1938. Nazi groups supporting the regimes of Hitler and Mussolini were causing increasing civil unrest in Austria. Intense pressure was put on the moderate

Austrian leader, Kurt von Schuschnigg, who eventually resigned. His successor, a carefully-chosen Nazi, Artur Seyss-Inquart, invited a German occupation. Hitler, pleased with the rapturous reception he received from the Austrian people as he followed his armoured cars into Vienna, reversed the Versailles Treaty and unified the two countries.

His attention now turned to Czechoslovakia. The country had been created by the Paris conference in 1919 from a number of different national groups, which formed the eastern part of the country, and the prosperous Sudeten region in the west, which had formerly been part of Germany. As Sudeten produced 70% of the country's electricity, iron and steel, and was the location of crucial underground defences, it was no surprise that the Czechoslovakian Government was keen to retain the region. Hitler claimed the moral high ground, as the German-speaking people of the Sudeten wanted to revert to their mother country. If this could not be achieved diplomatically, he would use force. Czechoslovakia possessed one of the most respected armies in Europe, and more importantly had signed treaties with France and Russia, which agreed support in the event of an unprovoked attack. These, plus Britain's likely response, were the reasons for the opposition among Hitler's Generals.

Chamberlain attempted to take control of the situation. On 15 September 1938 he visited Hitler at his summer retreat in the Bavarian mountains. Hitler made it clear to the British Prime Minister that he intended to occupy Sudeten, one way or another. Chamberlain's reaction was his first critical mistake. He returned to London and convinced his Cabinet that Britain should persuade France to allow Germany to take control of their former lands in Czechoslovakia. In return an assurance was to be sought from Hitler that Germany would not occupy the remainder of the country and would commit to peace generally.

Having secured French support, the British Government organised a summit meeting to ratify a treaty, Chamberlain's second mistake. In addition to Hitler, and the French Prime Minister, Edouard Daladier, he chose to invite Benito Mussolini, but not Joseph Stalin or any representative from Russia. The meeting took place on 29-30 September, at the headquarters of the Nazi party in Munich. As a process of negotiation it was a triumph for Hitler. He emerged with more Czechoslovakian territory than he had demanded of Chamberlain two weeks previously; in return he gave only vague reassurances that he had no intention of keeping.

It is difficult to know if Hitler was bluffing over Czechoslovakia, or what would have happened had Chamberlain taken a tougher line. On the balance of probability, if Britain and France had made it clear they would go to war over the Sudeten issue, Hitler might have faced revolt by his Generals had he ordered an invasion. By excluding Russia, Britain and France missed the opportunity of forming a powerful triumvirate which may have prevented a major war. Hitler proceeded to take full advantage of the soured relationship between Russia and the two western European powers.

Although Britain had sold Czechoslovakia down the river, Chamberlain made the most of the situation, arriving back at London's Heston Airport, waving the paper Hitler had signed, and claiming 'peace in our time'. The Prime Minister was too astute a politician to really believe this spin-doctoring, but he knew it had bought more precious time for Britain's rearmament programme.

★

The primary contract to build the biggest factory in the British Isles was awarded to Gee Walker & Slater Ltd. The completion target was June 1940. By the beginning of 1939 Great Western Railways had already laid most of the 24 miles of track that would be used to bring empty steel shells into the factory complex, and take out the explosive-filled bombs and ammunition. At this stage the railway lines were being used to deliver 12 million bricks, concrete sufficient to cover four square miles, and a vast array of benching and assembly equipment. In all, the site would require 58 miles of roadway, 300 miles of electrical cabling, 20 miles of water piping and 64 miles of sewage pipe-work.

Many of the 1,110 buildings were of a type of construction that could withstand explosion. Most of the designs shared the same small windows, placed high in the walls to avoid injury by glass in the event of an accident. Work was already underway on Tremains Halt Railway Station, larger than most London commuter terminals, and a bus station big enough to serve a large town.

Over at Island Farm twenty-two Nissen Huts, each capable of accommodating a hundred people, were erected to house workers from outlying areas. Towns as far away as Carmarthen and Chepstow were deemed to be within the recruitment radius required to find the 40,000 employees required.

Meanwhile, at the north side of the adjacent Brackla ridge, work had begun on the network of storage tunnels. Copying engineering used on parts of the London Underground system, each of the seven tunnels constructed had its own railway platform and a series of spurs, going deeper into the hill, that were to be used for longer-term storage. All the entrances were approached via long man-made gullies, designed to minimise the effect of a directly aimed bomb. By now it was known that south Wales would be within the range of enemy bombers.

In February 1939, with work on schedule, disaster struck. A fire broke out in a completed building, designated to be part of the arsenal's printing works, and being used during the construction process by planning staff. Fortunately, as fire engines from Bridgend and nearby towns rushed to the scene, the skeleton fire brigade that had already been employed, and which would form a permanent protection unit when the factory was operational, was attempting to deal with the blaze. The fire was brought under control before it could spread, but not before vital plans and blueprints were destroyed. Sabotage was originally suspected but eventually ruled out by the Police. As the fateful events of 1939 unfolded in Europe, the Government decided that the building programme needed to be accelerated. The estimated cost of £4.6 million shot up to £7.2 million. The immediate problem was finding an extra 550 carpenters and 600 bricklayers.

*

Whereas supporters of appeasement could rationalise Germany's action in respect of Austria and the Sudeten as mere reversals of the Versailles Treaty, Hitler's next move was one of blatant aggression. Reneging completely on the Munich agreement, he ordered German tanks into the Czech capital, Prague. A week later he demanded the return of Danzig and the Polish Corridor and announced Germany would no longer be bound by the 1935 naval agreement with Britain. Still not ready for war, Chamberlain's options for response were severely limited. An Anglo-French alliance was quickly agreed and the two countries offered assurances of protection, not only to Poland but also to Romania, Greece, Turkey, Holland, Switzerland and Denmark. Given how hollow Britain's assurances to Czechoslovakia had been, it is no surprise how little credibility these guarantees were given: the latter three countries rejected them out of hand.

Hitler's response was to brief his military to prepare for a full-scale invasion of Poland. The dissent among his Generals had subsided to rumbling discontent. With eight months of rearmament, and the outdated Polish Army not perceived to be as challenging as the Czechs, any prospect of Hitler being overthrown had evaporated. Mussolini, also keen to expand, took advantage of Anglo-French assistance overlooking Albania, and Italian troops proceeded to occupy the country. The following month, on 22 May, Hitler and Mussolini signed their so-called 'Pact of Steel,' in which both countries agreed to aid each other in the event of an offensive or defensive war in Europe.

Russia was, as it had been for years, the pivotal factor in how events could unfold in Europe. The British Government had made a crucial mistake in not involving Stalin in the Czech crisis. The Russian leader now found his support being courted by both Chamberlain and Hitler, but the way Britain handled its relationship with Russia during 1939 was to be Chamberlain's third error. The Prime Minister was under increasing pressure from Parliament to enter into an alliance with Stalin as a matter of urgency. Chamberlain was not convinced. He found Communism fundamentally abhorrent and did not trust Russia or its leader. He knew that Britain remained far from ready for war and felt that a British-Russian alliance was more likely to provoke than deter Hitler. Publicly, Chamberlain had firmly embraced a policy of appeasement: any u-turn would appear personally humiliating. Arguments about how confident he really was in this policy, as opposed to merely relying on the strategy to buy time, has occupied commentators for many years. In respect of this latest crisis, it appears he genuinely believed that Germany and Poland would settle the issue of Danzig by negotiation.

Placing most pressure on Chamberlain was Winston Churchill. Dismissed as a political has-been, Churchill increasingly struck a chord with the British public. In May 1939, Chamberlain succumbed to the pressure and agreed to enter into negotiations with Russia. The result was a diplomatic disaster. Chamberlain should have travelled to Russia personally, to build the crucial bridge with Stalin that was necessary after shutting him out of the Munich agreement. An alliance could have been formed and the small print left to be agreed after Hitler's reaction had been gauged.

Instead a junior diplomatic delegation, led by the spectacularly named, but low ranking Admiralty official, Sir Reginald Aylmer Ranfurly Plunkett-Ernie-Erle-Drax, was dispatched to Russia. Even their mode of transport, a merchant steamship that took six days to arrive, implied a lack of urgency. Sir Reginald had no power to agree any alliance and not surprisingly, by the end of August, the talks had spluttered to a halt. The last remaining opportunity to avoid a full-scale war in Europe had been lost.

Within days, Hitler made his move. A Nazi-Soviet pact was agreed that not only prevented the two powers going to war against each other, but also divided Poland between them. The British Government was astounded; it had believed Hitler would never accept the ideology of Communism. This was naivety of the first degree as after Czechoslovakia it should have been apparent that Hitler would agree to anything that allowed him to achieve his aims.

Having weathered the possibility of being overthrown by his Generals, Hitler, flushed with his success in Czechoslovakia, and now confident that Germany was prepared for war, had already decided his course of action. The previous May, in an address to his Generals, he had announced his intention to occupy Poland in order to give Germany the 'living space' it needed. He did not believe that Britain and France would respond but if they did then they would be attacked. The Generals were not as confident in their current military capacity as Hitler, but the Polish Army, still reliant on horse mounted cavalry, was considered inferior to the modern German military.

Following the breakdown of negotiations between Britain and Russia, and the resulting alliance he had entered into with Stalin, Hitler addressed his Generals again in August. By now there could be no ambiguity as to his intentions. Not only was Poland to be occupied, it was to be crushed and repopulated. Hitler was adamant that Chamberlain, and Daladier, "those poor worms I experienced in Munich", would be too cowardly to attack.

The first victim of the Second World War was a common criminal, plucked out of prison by the Gestapo and taken to the frontier town of Gleiwitz, where he was shot. The body was dressed in a Polish uniform and placed in the local radio station. On Friday 1 September 1939, the day after this 'attack', German tanks rolled into Poland.

Chamberlain immediately demanded withdrawal, but knew his policy of appeasement was finally at an end. The Prime Minister used a radio broadcast the following Sunday to announce that Britain was at war with Germany. In Bridgend, the munitions factory was a year away from full capacity, but six months ahead of schedule, the production lines began to roll out their bombs.

3. CODE OF HONOUR

The dormitory buildings being built as temporary accommodation for the workers assembling the bombs in Bridgend would also provide the setting for the final stage of the military career of Hitler's most respected General, a man who epitomised the culture, honour and traditions of the German Army: a convention that the Fuhrer was about to desecrate.

Karl Rudolf Gerd von Rundstedt was born on 12 December 1875 in the ancient town of Aschersleben on the eastern slopes of the Harz Mountains. His family, which could be traced back to the twelfth century, was one of the most elite in Prussia. In addition to managing their estates, generations of the family pursued military careers, fighting beside William of Orange; helping the English dispose of Bonnie Prince Charlie; protecting European Protestantism and rallying behind the first King of Prussia. Gerd's great-great-grandfather served Frederick the Great. His great-grandfather was among the handful of Prussian officers that led a resurgent nation against Napoleon.

In a break with the tradition of marriage within the Prussian aristocracy, Gerd's father chose a French woman of Huguenot descent. From his mother the young Gerd learnt to speak fluent French. The family's English nanny added a third language. Although the boy demonstrated artistic talent, it was ordained that he would enter military school at an early age. Almost sixty years later Gerd would have ample opportunity to revisit his love of painting while a prisoner at Island Farm.

By the late nineteenth century, the von Rundstedt family no longer enjoyed a level of wealth commensurate with their heritage. Gerd, who was a gifted horseman before his tenth birthday, desperately wanted to join a cavalry regiment, but family finances meant that he had to settle for the infantry when he left Cadet College. The young man was indoctrinated in the strict Prussian code of honour that had evolved over centuries, and governed almost every aspect of officer life. Loyalty to the Kaiser was total, and the role of the military was to serve without question. In return, an officer was immune from civil justice, disciplining being a matter for the Army alone: someone who did not possess it himself could not try a man of honour. How the

Prussian code of honour was applied in the many gruesome events of the Second World War would become a core issue at the subsequent war crimes trials in Nuremberg. Rundstedt himself summed up part of it when giving evidence there: "It is a very ancient Prussian tradition that an officer does not concern himself with politics."

After marrying well in 1902, and progressing through the ranks to considerable praise and commendation from everyone under whom he served, von Rundstedt was given his first command in 1912. It was not an easy posting. Captain von Rundstedt was put in charge of the Alsace region. Traditionally a contentious fault-line between German and France, the area was particularly volatile as the great European powers slid toward war. Von Rundstedt's understanding of the French helped him keep a lid on matters and prompted his promotion to the Chief of Operations of an Infantry Division.

Within weeks of his new appointment war was declared and he soon saw his first active service in Belgium. Here he tasted victory, to be followed by frustration. After the initial success of occupying Brussels the German Army became bogged down as it advanced towards Paris. Von Rundstedt's frustration with the conduct of the campaign by his senior commanders would remain with him. When he found himself in their position, in the same place with the same objectives twenty-six years later, he would not emulate their mistakes.

On 28 November 1914 von Rundstedt was promoted to Major and awarded the Iron Cross First Class for his endeavours. Although he was not wounded during the campaign his health was bad, and he served out the first winter of the war in the relative comfort of Antwerp. Germany had now opened up an eastern front and, at the beginning of 1915; von Rundstedt was transferred to the Polish capital of Warsaw, the city already being under German occupation.

Hostilities against Russia would last another three years, during which von Rundstedt laid the foundations of his military reputation. He was cited for 'daringly executed raids', and bringing about 'outstanding success consequent in the enormous bounty of liberated territories.' He was also enormously popular with both the men who served under him and his peers. Even in war his sense of humour shone through: he was a particularly good mimic.

German successes were not mirrored on the Western Front. Von Rundstedt was transferred to Alsace during the final few months of the war and watched from a distance as the German Army was brought to its knees. History would note that it marked the end for the old regime. At the time it created an uncertain future for its officers.

Military pride initially remained intact, but as the victorious diplomats exerted their revenge on Germany at Versailles, the country plummeted into anarchy and chaos. Any Prussian hopes of opposing the draconian terms of the treaty were quickly dashed. Von Rundstedt remained part of the skeleton Army that Germany retained. He was now a Lieutenant Colonel and ironically he achieved his boyhood ambition when he was appointed Chief of Staff to a cavalry division.

The years immediately after the Great War were relatively sedate for von Rundstedt. His diminished role allowed him to spend time with his wife and son. The riding skills he learnt as a boy were put to recreational, not military, use as he excelled as a cross-country event rider, although an accident fractured his hip and left him with a large scar on his lower left cheek. Further promotions took him to the rank of Major General by 1927. The following year he proudly took command of the 2nd Cavalry Division.

As Hitler began his rise to power, and the dignity of the German military was slowly restored, von Rundstedt began to adapt to the changing face of warfare. A colleague, Heinz Guderian, converted the traditionalist Prussian away from his beloved horse to the virtues of modern tanks and mobile armour. Von Rundstedt also took a particular interest in the blossoming radio technology.

While von Rundstedt and his Prussian peers took pleasure in the covert rebuilding of Germany's armed forces, a new spectre became increasingly apparent. The Nazi Party had its own separate militia, the S.A. When clandestine military exercises were held that would form the basis of *Blitzkrieg* tactics, Hitler demanded that his S.A officers take part. This order was met with dissatisfaction, though not dissent, from the military. Von Rundstedt was quickly aware that the interlopers came from a radically different culture.

Von Rundstedt was now based in Berlin, a city he described as a "pig-sty", where he had his first direct dealings with Hitler. He maintained a distance from his new masters, but as he saw it, they had achieved power legally and, regardless of personal opinion, it was not for the Army to oppose them. To the Army establishment, when Hitler became Chancellor he had effectively replaced the old Kaiser in constitutional terms. Leaders had changed many times over the years. The 'Night of the Long Knives', when it took place, was a matter between opposing forces within Hitler's party. The newly formed Gestapo was a government organisation, not part of the mainstream Army.

With Hitler firmly in power some military officers, although none with von Rundstedt's seniority, moved into the increasingly powerful S.S. For those soldiers, raised in the traditional culture of a different world, a wind of change was heading their way. First, a new pledge of allegiance was introduced into the armed forces that declared loyalty to "the Fuhrer of the German Reich and Commander-in-Chief of the Wehrmacht". Then the Nazi salute was introduced and uniforms were to display new insignia. A traditional Prussian phrase was being increasingly heard in the Officer's Mess that would resonate long after the forthcoming war ended: "Befehl ist Befehl" – orders are orders.

One of Hitler's first anti-Jewish policies was to make recruitment at officer level conditional on the applicant being able to prove 'pureness' of ancestry. In an unusual demonstration of his personal thoughts, von Rundstedt scrawled 'Aryan shit' across this particular file in his office.

Whatever von Rundstedt's opinion was of the direction Germany was taking, he assumed that the events were taking place in the twilight of a distinguished career. In 1935, on the occasion of his 60th birthday, Hitler presented a signed photograph to the man who was, by now, the second most senior Army officer in Germany. The following March, Rundstedt represented the German Army at the funeral of King George V. Having never visited London before, the veteran General was pleasantly surprised to be made an honourary member of the prestigious Malborough Club and to attend a banquet at Buckingham Palace. On his return, having experienced the British at first hand, von Rundstedt demonstrated a visionary insight into the potential outcome of a possible war. Addressing a meeting of staff officers von Rundstedt warned that "a Continental power wishing to defeat England must either have Russia or the United States as an ally in order to have any chance of victory."

At the beginning of 1938 Hitler had almost completed the strategy that would serve as the foundation for his dream of a thousand year Reich. He was widely adored by the German public. His control of the Nazi Party, and therefore government, was total. His inner circle of trustees could be counted on one hand. Through them his power base was protected and his policies implemented. The political game of chess played out in Europe and beyond since he came to power was moving increasingly in his favour. His military resources were nearly at a level that would permit offensive war. There was, however, one piece still to be put into place.

Heinrich Himmler's S.S. was now strong enough to assure not only Hitler's political status, but also to implement his plans. When war came, this Army-within-an-Army would carry out the same role inside Germany's new territories. Hitler needed the right person at the head of the mainstream Army who would command the respect of those beneath him, while maintaining unswerving loyalty to the Fuhrer.

The Commander-in-Chief of the German Army, and von Rundstedt's superior and close friend, was General Werner von Fritsch. On 27 January 1938, von Rundstedt was summoned to a meeting with Hitler at the Chancellery. Aware that von Fritsch was on leave in Egypt at the time, von Rundstedt did not foresee anything untoward. He found Hitler in a state of high agitation. Himmler had presented the Fuhrer with a dossier proving, beyond doubt, that von Fritsch was a practising homosexual. Von Rundstedt dismissed the accusation out of hand, prompting Hitler to justify his case by pointing out that if the allegation was untrue, then when confronted with it von Fritsch should have angrily denied it. Instead he had displayed an ice-cold reserve. Von Rundstedt pointed out that, as a nobleman, this was the only way in which von Fritsch should have reacted. The General stood his ground. He felt that the accusations were ludicrous, and in any event the only judicial tribunal before which von Fritsch could be tried was a military Court of Honour.

Hitler conceded the point of law but was adamant that von Fritsch should be removed immediately as Commander-in-Chief, which von Rundstedt recognised was the Fuhrer's prerogative. Hitler sought his advice as to Fritsch's replacement. Von Rundstedt had no desire for the job and was relieved that Hitler had not considered him. He was never a candidate, as Hitler knew he had no loyalty towards the Nazi Party.

The Fuhrer's first suggestion was Walther von Reichenau and he asked von Rundstedt for a candid opinion. He gave it, turning von Reichenau down "in the name of the entire Army". Hitler's next choice, Walther von Brauchitsch, was much more acceptable to von Rundstedt. Fourteen years his junior, von Brauchitsch was 'old-school', part of a traditional Prussian family with a Guards Corp background. What von Rundstedt did not know was that von Brauchitsch was about to marry a fanatical Nazi woman, freed from his first marriage with the sum of 80,000 Reichmarks personally provided by Hitler.

At the end of the meeting von Rundstedt broached the question of his own future. He was now sixty-three and felt that the time had come to retire. Hitler took pains to praise his loyalty and service. He asked von Rundstedt if he would remain for another six months, and return thereafter if there was an emergency. Von Rundstedt agreed, not realising that such an emergency would last for six years and end with him sharing a prisoner of war camp with the man he had just endorsed for the most senior post in the German Army.

Within a month, his colleagues had acquitted von Fritsch. Himmler, it seemed, had mixed him up with another officer in a case of mistaken identity. Nevertheless, von Fritsch was not to be reinstated, a decision he was forced to accept as an officer. His way of dealing with Himmler, however, was a classic Prussian soldier's solution. He would regain his honour from the head of the S.S. in a duel; the challenge administered, as custom dictated, through his old friend Gerd von Rundstedt. The elderly General was able, instead, to defuse the situation, the first of many decisions and actions von Rundstedt would take that would have a pivotal effect on millions of lives.

As the crisis in Czechoslovakia broke, von Brauchitsch had his first opportunity to repay Hitler. A meeting of all senior Generals was called for 4 August, which von Rundstedt attended as the impending emergency had delayed his retirement. The consensus was that Germany was not ready to go to war but von Brauchitsch managed to defuse what verged on a military revolt, promising personally to make known their concerns to Hitler.

A breakaway group of officers pursued a more drastic course of action, to the point of sending an emissary, Major Eward von Kleist-Schmenzin, to London. Churchill, still in the political wilderness, received him warmly. Not so Chamberlain, who said the group of German officers reminded him of "the Jacobites at the Court of France", and dismissed what von Kleist-Schmenzin had to say as being unreliable. The plotters felt that von Rundstedt would support them, but his view was that a coup would not be supported by the rank and file, which, at that point, still considered Hitler to be the saviour of Germany. As it transpired, with Chamberlain and his government backing down over the issue of Czechoslovakia, any potential coup became academic.

Von Rundstedt at last retired with his family to their home in Kassel. Hitler's parting gift to the distinguished officer was to appoint him as Honourary Colonel of the 18th Infantry Regiment, a position von Rundstedt greatly appreciated. His retirement, however, was to be short lived.

4. HITLER'S GENERAL

When Hitler had made his intentions in respect of Poland clear to the military hierarchy he called for detailed invasion plans. The task was entrusted to General Gerd von Rundstedt. With an array of motorised armour, and an air force of fast single-wing planes, war would be different. By the time that Stalin and Hitler were in agreement over Poland, and German strategy could be finalised, von Rundstedt had already dreamed up a totally different concept of warfare: *Blitzkrieg.*

From the moment that the order to commence invasion was given the antiquated Polish Army was helpless as waves of Luftwaffe fighters and dive-bombers blasted a passage through the defending troops. What followed on land was an Army, travelling aboard light tanks and armoured vehicles, moving across the flat Polish grasslands at a pace never before seen. Resistance that survived the aerial and motorised attacks was swept up by old-fashioned infantry troops in the rear. Within ten days of the German Army crossing the border, the Poles were reduced to rearguard defences of the capital Warsaw and the southeastern city of Lvov. When, on 17 September, the Russian Army invaded from the east, Poland's fate was sealed. The garrison in Warsaw fought on bravely but hopelessly for another ten days, before constant German bombing forced its surrender.

As von Rundstedt and his officers dissected the success of their new style of war, and Hitler was drawing up a new border dividing Poland between Germany and Russia across a line from East Prussia to the Carpathian Mountains, ominous events were taking place behind the German front line. Three S.S. regiments, consisting of 24,000 men, followed the fast advancing main Army, apparently with orders to enforce 'police and security measures'. Daubed in white paint on the side of one of the railway carriages carrying these men a slogan carried a chilling, prophetic message: "We're off to Poland to thrash the Jews".

At the small Polish town of Truskolasy, on September 3, the day that Britain declared war on Germany, 55 Polish peasants, including a child of two, were rounded up in the market place and slaughtered. At nearby Wieruszow, twenty Jews were assembled in the centre of the town for execution. As the German front closed in on Warsaw, similar atrocities were continuing across occupied Poland. When protests were made from the regular Army, Hitler promptly summoned von Brauchitsch to his temporary headquarters on board his private train, 'Amerika'. Here Hitler gave the order that the Army was to "abstain from interfering" in S.S. operations.

On 21 September, the senior S.S. officer Reinhard Heydrich called a meeting of his commanders in Berlin. Here he made it clear that the execution of Hitler's "ultimate aim" in respect of people not considered fit to be part of the Third Reich, would take a "prolonged period of time" and must be kept "strictly secret." The following month Hitler signed an amnesty for those S.S. men arrested in Poland by the Army for offences against civilians. Six years later, the Nuremberg war crimes trial would have to decide on two issues: who did what, and who knew what?

Quite how Britain and France, which had now also declared war on Germany, intended to assist Poland, became academic with the astonishing speed of the German occupation. Any hope that Britain's main ally from the previous war would become involved again was dashed when US President Franklin D. Roosevelt, despite 28 Americans being among the first naval casualties of the war when the passenger liner *Athenia* was sunk, declared: "Let no man or woman thoughtlessly or falsely talk of America sending its armies to European fields. At this moment there is being prepared a proclamation of American neutrality".

As Russia proceeded to launch a massive military assault on Finland, the British, French and German leaders assessed the dramatic events of the autumn of 1939. A half-hearted French advance towards the Ruhr coalfields had not troubled the superior German defences. Britain, using a Swedish intermediary, Birger Dahlerus, had suggested to Germany that both fortification of the new frontier with Russia, and the return of all pre-Versailles colonies, were now acceptable. Hitler's reaction was to issue a directive commanding his military chiefs to draw up an offensive to attack Western Europe.

The Fuhrer had no intention of observing his pact with Russia longer than was necessary; his concern was that Stalin would break it first. With Britain building massive munitions factories, Hitler was now fully aware of its rearmament programme, and feared that within a few months a combined Anglo-French Army would pose a real threat to Germany's western frontier. The majority of his Generals did not share Hitler's confidence in the tactics of *Blitzkrieg*. The military consensus was that German combined forces were not sufficiently strong enough to invade France, let alone Britain, and that any further aggression would lead to a world war with fatal consequences for Germany. A coup was suggested, led again by General Halder, but without the support of General Friedrich Fromm, the Commander in Chief of Home Forces, and with Hitler having now gained the trust of the rank and file, the plot was aborted.

Hitler set the date of the invasion of France for 12 November 1939, but now met with a force that even he could not control: the weather. With no abatement of the adverse conditions into December, and with the Fuhrer allowing Christmas leave, the invasion was delayed to 17 January. Fate was to intervene, initially against Germany, but ultimately, and ironically against the Western Allies. On 10 January 1940 a plane en route between Munster and Bonn, carrying a liaison officer along with the complete operational plans to attack the west, was forced off course by bad weather and crashed in Belgium. German High Command had no alternative but to assume the plans had fallen into Allied hands. Hitler was persuaded that an entirely new campaign needed to be planned.

The original strategy was based on Army Group 'B', led by General Max Bock, who had played a supporting role in Poland, spearheading the main thrust through central Belgium. Von Rundstedt's Army Group 'A' would provide back up from the east, with a secondary offensive through the densely wooded, and hilly Ardennes region. The Generals, all veterans of the Great War, harboured reservations that this attack was too reminiscent of the Schlieffen Plan, and feared a similar outcome with the Germany Army at best making slow progress south, and ultimately being ground to a halt on the Somme. Hitler, on the other hand, was confident this would not be the fate of his modern *Blitzkrieg*.

The Chief of Staff, Erich von Manstein approached von Rundstedt with an alternative idea. Twelve years von Rundstedt's junior, von Manstein had been a low-ranking officer during the previous war and despite steadily rising through the ranks during the years in which the German Army was rebuilt, his rank did not place him in the inner sanctum of decision makers. Von Rundstedt, however, was willing to hear von Manstein's plan, which was based on the time-honoured theory of doing the opposite of what the enemy expects.

Von Manstein had seen first hand how the new lightly armoured machinery, key to *Blitzkrieg*, had functioned under battle conditions in Poland. Taking advice from a colleague who knew the terrain of eastern Belgium, von Manstein was confident that with increased resources a lightening move could be made through the Ardennes forest that would take Allied defences completely by surprise. With the Allies' main defences geared for an expected invasion further north, von Rundstedt's attack would face soft opposition and, with General Bock's Army making their move at the same time, a classic pincer movement would be completed.

Von Rundstedt took the plan forward to von Brauchitsch and Halder at High Command. It was dismissed out of hand, but von Rundstedt persisted and arranged for von Manstein to meet with Hitler, who was enthusiastic and immediately claimed the idea as his own. High Command had no choice but to accept the strategy.

The original German documents had, in fact, survived the air crash and were in the hands of the Allies, who were pondering whether they had been deliberately planted. Their conclusion was that there was no feasible alternative to the only logical offensive. Military historians now believe that if Germany had proceeded with their original plan, either in late 1939, or when the invasion actually happened in May 1940, the German advance would indeed have ground to a halt on the fields of northern France.

While this military chess game was being plotted in Western Europe, British and German eyes were also on Scandinavia. Finland had succumbed to Russia; Denmark was felt to be a soft target, but would only be of use as part of a wider northern European strategy. Norway was considered vital to all sides, as its naval bases were crucial to both the North Atlantic routes and the Arctic shipping lanes in and out of Russia and Eastern Europe. Sweden was a mass producer of iron ore, critical to any war effort. With the exception of Finland, overtaken by events, the remaining Scandinavian countries had immediately declared neutrality at the start of the war.

Britain's new First Lord of the Admiralty, Winston Churchill, was under no illusion that a German invasion of Norway was both inevitable and imminent. Apart from naval benefits, it would also place Luftwaffe bombers in closer range to Britain. Churchill argued to his War Cabinet colleagues that if the Norwegian Government could not be persuaded to invite a British occupation, then the country must be invaded by force. British invasion plans were well advanced when they were made redundant by a typical piece of Hitlerian opportunism.

The Fuhrer had not planned to expand the theatre of war and was content with Norway's neutrality, although he was in discussion with Vidkun Quisling, the former Norwegian Minister of Defence. Quisling led a small Nazi party that he felt, with German support, could mount a coup and establish a puppet government. When Hitler learned of the advanced British plans to occupy Norway he ordered an invasion on 9 April 1940. Although Norwegian underground resistance would continue throughout the war, occupation was complete within two weeks. For good measure Germany had also occupied Denmark, giving Hitler control of the entrance to the Baltic and effectively curtailing the supply of Swedish iron ore to Britain.

With the advent of spring Germany was now set to implement von Manstein's plan. In the meantime Chamberlain's wounded premiership was brought to an end. On 10 May, as Winston Churchill was installed as Prime Minister, German tanks thrust through western defences into Holland, Belgium and France.

Earlier in the day the Luftwaffe had crippled the Dutch capital of The Hague and the country's major port, Rotterdam. German armoured forces raced across the border, taking less than five days to place Holland under Nazi rule. To the south, General Bock's Army Group B swarmed into Belgium, securing every main bridge across the country's network of canals and rivers. As more and more Allied troops were committed to countering the invading forces, von Rundstedt's Army Group A delivered the telling blow through the Ardennes. After coping with the supposedly impassable terrain exactly as von Manstein had envisaged, von Rundstedt's flank took less than four days to emerge over the French border and cross the strategically important River Meuse.

By the time the two advancing German armies joined up, the Allies were in disarray. On 15 May, the new French Prime Minister, Paul Reynaud, telephoned his British counterpart to say they had lost the battle. Churchill, with almost 400,000 troops in northern France, immediately ordered the British Expeditionary Force to retreat towards the coastal town of Dunkirk. Frantic arrangements were made for a full-scale naval evacuation, while German forces moved west to cut off the retreating Army.

Throughout the course of the Second World War all sides made pivotal diplomatic, strategic and military errors. The decision about to be made by von Rundstedt and Hitler, in terms of the consequences had it not been taken, was without doubt the most significant example of the latter. On the evening of 21 May, with the British troops moving desperately towards Dunkirk, von Rundstedt, on his own initiative, gave the order for the pursuing German divisions to halt. The following morning, Hitler visited von Rundstedt at the General's temporary headquarters in Charleville, near the eastern extreme of the Franco-Belgian border. Hitler was elated with events of the previous two weeks. Rundstedt was already thinking of the move south to complete the invasion of France. He stressed to Hitler that both his, and General Bock's armies, which had achieved such spectacular success, needed to rest and regroup. He argued that the pace of a *Blitzkrieg* operation could only be maintained for a short period. Hitler agreed entirely that conserving resources for future operations was of paramount importance and personally endorsed the order to halt all French-based forces. Discussion between the men turned to a southern offensive to "settle matters with the French". To the amazement of Army commanders in the west, orders came through from General Command that "Dunkirk would be left to the Luftwaffe".

The flotilla of small boats, shuttling across the channel between the ports of southern England and the beaches of Dunkirk is one of the abiding images of the War. The halting of German land forces bemused the British command but allowed their beleaguered Army to reach the coast. Now, despite sustained air attack, 338,000 troops would be evacuated to safety. Had the evacuees of Dunkirk been killed, or taken prisoner, it is difficult to see how Britain could have shaped the outcome of the war as it did. It was out of character for Hitler to allow mistakes to go unpunished, but in this instance there was little recrimination. It may be that the decision, which Hitler accepted as his own, was arrived at by a combination of von Rundstedt's advice, an underestimation on the number of British troops, and an over reliance on the Luftwaffe. Another theory, backed in later years by Generals critical of Hitler's preference for aggression over diplomacy, points to Hitler still intending, even at this stage of the war, to reach peace with Britain. The loss of the Expeditionary Force would have made this impossible.

Von Rundstedt's promotion to the rank of *Generalfeldmarschall*, and his instruction to prepare plans to invade Britain, reveals that the General had not been held to account for his advice. Nor does it support the notion that Hitler hankered after peace, although he could have been seeking to further strengthen his position. In any event, the next German priority was to defeat the French.

As though their only hope rested in history, the French defensive line was laid along the River Somme. However, with a half defeated, demoralised Army, and only minimal British support now remaining, the outcome was inevitable. It took the German offensive four days to break through, prompting Reynaud and his Government to withdraw from Paris. Encouraged by German success Mussolini declared war on France the following day. A further four days later, on 14 June, German tanks drove up the Champs Elysees, while the remaining French defence had been pushed as far south as the River Rhône. With the intention of installing a compliant government, Hitler decided to draw a line of occupation, and demonstrating a gift for irony, made the French sign his armistice terms in the same railway coach, in the same location, as Germany had signed its surrender in 1918.

Despite his publicly stated hopes for peace with Britain, Hitler was demanding of his Generals an immediate invasion of England. Von Rundstedt weighed up the fact that the German military were trained in seaborne landings against the current state of the British Army, which had abandoned so much of its arms and equipment on the beaches at Dunkirk. As troop barges could be quickly arranged, and basic training hastily provided, von Rundstedt concluded that his Fuhrer's ambition could be accommodated.

He drew up a plan, codenamed Sealion, based on stretching the British around their southern coastline from Ramsgate, on the easternmost tip of Kent, to Lyme Bay in the west. After securing cross-channel bridgeheads, the now tried and tested *Blitzkrieg* would be used to capture high ground along an arc from the Thames Estuary to Portsmouth, while another attack moved northwards from Dorset to the River Severn. London would be cut off from the west.

Von Rundstedt's plans hit a problem when he consulted with his naval opposite number, Admiral Erich Raeder on 31 July. Raeder, who held the British Fleet in high regard, was not confident that the German Navy could provide the necessary cover for such a wide area. He advocated a much narrower corridor across the Channel, and only if air cover could be assured. Rundstedt and Raeder were relieved of having to make a final decision as Goering had assured Hitler that the Luftwaffe could drive the R.A.F. out of the sky in advance of any invasion. Hitler reluctantly put off the invasion until mid-September while Goering accomplished this.

The Battle of Britain began on 10 August. It was won, not only by the bravery of the British fighter pilots, but also through the superior technology of British radar, the skill of anti-aircraft crews, and the efforts of the aircraft industry to produce planes almost as quickly as they were being lost. As the battle raged above southern England and the Channel, Hitler was forced into a series of delays until, on 12 October 1940, Operation Sealion was postponed until the following spring. Hitler's attention turned to the east, leaving the Luftwaffe to bomb civilian Britain into submission.

With Western Europe under Nazi rule, its cities being subjected to heavy German bombing, no prospect of direct intervention from America, and the vital northern Atlantic supply lines taking horrendous losses, this was to be Britain's 'darkest hour'.

5. WALES AT WAR

On 24 August 1940 a Luftwaffe plane, approaching low over the Bristol Channel, banked slowly over Bridgend and circled the Royal Ordinance Factory. The clear conditions were perfect for reconnaissance, and with his cameraman's job quickly completed the pilot turned the plane south and headed back to France. The following day, German Bomber Command was poring over four detailed photographs of a prime target.

The original date for output at the arsenal to commence had been March, but as the Luftwaffe were taking their pictures the factory had been running at full production since September 1939. Nothing could disguise the magnitude of the site. It was the size of a small town, complete with its own hospital, Police Force, Fire Service, Bomb Disposal Unit, and Air Raid Wardens.

Three times a day, as shifts changed, a fleet of 144 buses and ten railway trains ferried the workers in and out. The 40,000 workforce was predominantly young women in their late teens and early twenties. Despite many having their men folk away at war, few chose to stay at the purpose-built dormitory accommodation at Island Farm, preferring instead to make arduous daily journeys to and from home.

Security at the complex was tight, as the greatest threat was not perceived to be from aerial bombing but German sabotage on the ground. As the workers arrived, random searches were made to ensure the strict bans on cigarettes and hairclips were adhered to. No smoking was an obvious safety precaution, but there was also a real danger from metal hairclips creating a fatal spark that could kill hundreds. The distinctive uniform of a munitions worker, a gown, turban, and rubber overshoes, again to avoid sparks, was donned in the many 'Shifting Houses', near the main entrances.

In Britain, unlike Germany, working in the munitions industry was not mandatory. The dangerous work was undertaken for a combination of patriotism – underwritten by the massive propaganda campaign to help the Home Front – and high wages. Many women there earned as much as £3 a week, more than their husbands or boyfriends serving in the forces, or working in the local collieries.

Although every precaution was taken for the safety of workers, conditions in the factory were tough, and the work repetitive. The bulk of the labour force sat at benches filling empty shells with explosives, which were then taken to more skilled workers who completed the delicate task of adding springs and detonators before the primed ammunition was taken away for storage. The day-to-day dangers were accepted as a way of life, but the main worker complaint resulted from the bright yellow dye added to the cordite explosive to make it clearly visible. Munitions workers could always be spotted on the streets, as their hands, faces and even teeth were permanently yellow. Women complained that the dye turned blonde hair green, and black hair orange. More serious was the number of skin complaints, treated at the on-site medical centre.

Although trade unions were banned there was a great camaraderie amongst the workers. Morale was maintained by piped radio playing the B.B.C.'s 'Music While You Work' programmes and 'ITMA', the comedy show that became a national institution. However, among the prevailing black humour there was also an inevitable tension created when people work in a powder keg.

From the beginning of the war there was a press ban on reporting factory accidents in the munitions and other high security industries, but by all accounts Bridgend enjoyed an exemplary safety record until 18 May 1941. The Sunday afternoon shift heading for shop 3G9 had been delayed by a problem with the doors at their Shifting House. The heavy sealed doors, sometimes doubled on high risk buildings, were a feature of the arsenal. This would normally have annoyed the shift's Senior Overlooker but today it allowed her to sort out a discrepancy with her colleague from the previous shift. The number of fuses loaded into primed bombs did not tally with the number remaining for the new shift. Eventually they agreed that 3,475 remained for the afternoon shift, a high target.

As the shifts were switching over, a maintenance team of carpenters arrived to make repairs to the linoleum floor around one of the workbenches. Maintenance work was not permitted when the shops were operational because of the danger of sparks, and in order to avoid closing one down, small jobs were completed during the change of shifts.

Audrey Matthews, Georgina McEllagott and Olive Bugler, all kitted out in their gowns, turbans, and rubber shoes made their way to their shop, not particularly bothered that they were late because of the jammed door. The girls were skilled workers, their job being to add detonators to explosive-filled bombs. Olive, at 19, was especially young to be on such a team. They were surprised to see two carpenters still working in their shop though pleased to see some new faces.

As usual, their Supervisor, Mrs Wilding, gave the girls a tray of detonators, and after being assured by the carpenters that they had almost finished, left to visit another shop. As usual, Olive took 50 detonators and passed the tray onto Audrey, sitting in the middle of the three girls. The subsequent Board of Enquiry concluded that it was at this point something caused an explosion. Olive was killed instantly but Audrey, who took the full brunt of the blast, and Georgina, on her other side, were still alive when the medical team arrived. Their injuries were too severe to be treated at the factory's medical centre and they were rushed to Bridgend General Hospital. Audrey survived for only four hours. Georgina hung on for four days before she too died.

There would be further fatalities at the Bridgend arsenal, and other workers would suffer serious injury, but for the management there was a growing fear of receiving a direct hit from the increasing Luftwaffe bombardment. The events of the second half of May 1940 had turned the war on its head. All of Britain had fallen in the range of German bombers, and a full-scale invasion, inconceivable prior to the occupation of Western Europe, seemed inevitable. Civil defence plans were urgently revised.

On 14 May, with Allied defeat in France already looming, the Secretary of State for War, Anthony Eden, appealed on the radio for volunteers to join the newly formed Local Defence Volunteers. The Government was hoping for 150,000 men to join this unpaid force. Within 24 hours, a quarter of a million men had come forward, joined by another 150,000 during the next two weeks and rising to one and a half million in total by the end of June.

The Home Guard, as it quickly became known, was comprised of men who were either in jobs deemed vital to the war effort or too young or too old to join the armed forces. Many were veterans of the First World War. It was intended that this force would provide back up, and in many areas front line defence against the expected invasion. With the regular Army insufficiently armed following the hasty retreat from France, the Home Guard was unarmed for almost a year. Had von Rundstedt's crack Western Army succeeded in crossing the Channel in 1940, it would have faced a defence force armed with an array of old hunting rifles, kitchen knives and broom handles.

As von Rundstedt planned Operation Sealion, British Commanders tried to second guess German strategy. It was anticipated that the main bridgehead would be across the narrowest stretch of the English Channel, on the Kent coast. If von Rundstedt's plan to invade along the entire south coast had been foreseen the British, doubtless, would have drawn the same conclusion as Admiral Raeder: that it was impossible without having first secured the crucial air supremacy fought out during the autumn of 1940. One potential German option considered likely was a secondary invasion via the coast of south Wales. If successful the Germans would control the vital ports of Swansea, Cardiff and possibly Bristol, as well as knocking out the Bridgend arsenal. From there the occupying Army would be well positioned to move eastwards towards London. Defences along the coast from Porthcawl to Barry were quickly reinforced with look-out posts, anti-aircraft guns and concrete 'pill boxes'.

With increased German bombing other home defence forces were needed. Plans were already in place for London and the Home Counties which now needed to be rolled out to all other parts of the country as quickly as possible. The Air Raid Warden Service was responsible for ensuring that black-out regulations were adhered to, and for shepherding the public into the network of bomb shelters built in major towns and cities. Auxiliary Fire Services and Police Corps were swiftly recruited. The Post Office formed special engineering units to effect immediate repairs to telephone and telex lines vital to air defence systems. All these volunteer forces would suffer terrible casualties over the following three years.

Most of Britain would, at some stage of the war, come under attack from the Luftwaffe; every major city was targeted at one time or another. London would suffer the most, with thousands of civilian deaths, but Liverpool, Hull, Bristol, Belfast and most memorably, Coventry, would also endure brutal attention. However, outside of London, a prime German target area was south Wales. In addition to the massive Bridgend munitions works, Port Talbot, ten miles to the west, was the site of one of the largest steel plants in the United Kingdom. Eight miles south east of Bridgend was the important R.A.F. base of St Athan. South Wales was the largest coalfield in Britain and the ports of Newport, Cardiff, Penarth, Barry and Swansea, within fifty miles of each other, accounted for a third of Britain's dry cargo. Fifty miles west of Swansea was Pembroke Dock and Milford Haven, one of the largest natural harbours in the world.

On 20 June 1940 R.A.F. St Athan was bombed. The following day Bridgend had its first air raid warning. Six days later the first bombs fell on Swansea. On 29 June the Luftwaffe made its first targeted strike of the Port Talbot steelworks and returned two days later. The opening two days of July saw raids on the smaller steelworks at Margam, between Port Talbot and Bridgend.

Realising that anti-aircraft defence in the area was woefully unprepared, and with 3 July being a clear day, the Luftwaffe was confident enough to attempt a daylight raid on the Royal Ordinance Factory. At a quarter past midday thirteen bombs were dropped leaving craters five feet deep in the villages of Ewenny, a mile from the accommodation units at Island Farm, and in Laleston, on the other side of Bridgend. The munitions factory had been spared a direct hit but any relief quickly evaporated when the sirens sounded again at 5.40 pm. This time the planes swooped in from the north with another load of bombs. The first hit part of the main town with the remainder falling in a line towards the village of Merthyr Mawr and on to the sand dunes beyond. Again the factory was unscathed.

The respite that followed over the next week was brought to a shuddering halt when 70 bombers made a concerted attack on Swansea on 10 July, while a smaller number headed for Cardiff and Aberdare. The Germans targeted the Rhondda coalfield three days later, followed by another two days of raids on St Athan. By the time that the Battle of Britain started, south Wales had endured air raids on 25 out of the previous 50 days.

If Welsh people thought that the Luftwaffe's attention would now be taken up with the critical conflict in the skies above the south east of England, they were wrong. Only four days of August were free from air raids. Swansea, Port Talbot, and St Athan were again the main targets. There appear to have been two attacks aimed at Bridgend, on 22 and 23 of August, but on both occasions the bombs fell on the nearby town of Llantwit Major.

The first day of September saw a new style of air attack on Swansea. The Blitz was wave after wave of planes sweeping over an area, bombarding the same targets. It left 70 dead, and was the first time the tactic had been used on a British city. It served as a practice for 7 September when 300 bombers and more than 600 fighters made the first of many such attacks on London. During the remainder of the month there were regular raids on Swansea, sporadic attacks on the south Wales valleys and two raids on Bridgend, on the 17th and

28th. Again, despite the Luftwaffe's detailed reconnaissance photographs, the bombs fell on neighbouring villages.

At last the prolonged battle for air supremacy in south east England, and Hitler's demand for air resources elsewhere in Europe, brought a reduction in raids on south Wales, although there were six more during October and four in November. South Wales was battered but spared the carnage that might have resulted from six months bombardment. Worse, however, was to follow.

The new year of 1941 saw German bombers return to south Wales for seven days during January, concentrating for the first time on Cardiff, which on 2 January, was blitzed with the loss of 165 lives. The absence of air raid sirens for the first two weeks of February heralded the fiercest bombing of the war in Wales. For three consecutive nights from 19 February, waves of German bombers destroyed the centre of Swansea. Two hundred civilians were killed. Less frequent but more sustained raids appeared to be the Luftwaffe's new strategy. Cardiff suffered more attacks and considerable loss of life during March and April, but increasingly German air resource was being redirected to eastern Europe, and the prime target of the Bridgend munitions complex continued to elude the bombers.

On 12 March the arsenal was attacked again but once more the bombs fell wide of the target landing on Litchard, to the north of the town. Exactly a month later another strike missed, this time destroying the chapel and twelve houses in the village of Treoes, less than a mile to the east of the arsenal. Ten days later two bombs intended for the factory landed in a field three miles away. On 30 April, a dozen incendiary devices, more than capable of destroying the entire works, landed near to historic Coity Castle, half a mile to the north. The raids were becoming fewer, but there would be five more attempts to destroy the arsenal. The penultimate occurred on 2 July 1942 when bombs fell once again on the nearby villages of Merthyr Mawr, Ewenny and Litchard.

Swansea endured an unexpected blitz on 16 February 1943, and in April a lone bomber dived towards the arsenal but its load fell on St Mary Hill, two miles away. Quite how the biggest munitions factory in the country avoided the thousands of bombs that rained on south Wales for more than three years remains a mystery.

Nine hundred and eighty five Welsh civilians lost their lives to German bombs. Many thousands more suffered the same fate in London and throughout the British Isles. As the war continued,

British bombers began increasingly to subject German civilians to similar terror. A forty-three minute raid on 28 July 1943 killed 42,000 people in Hamburg. An estimated 60,000 were to perish in Dresden in March 1945.

The last German bomber flew over south Wales on 18 May 1943. The War was far from over, but the tide had begun to turn, very slowly, towards the Allies.

6. THE ONE THAT GOT AWAY

Around 600 B.C. the Chinese warrior Sun Tze proposed that limits should be imposed on the conduct of armies during warfare. Four hundred years later the notion of war crimes was included in the Hindu code of Manu. It took western civilisation until 1625 before the first written notion of humanitarian behaviour during war appeared in *On the Law of War and Peace* by Hugo Grotius. Although rules of military honour continued to evolve, nothing was formalised until Henri Dunant, founder of the Red Cross, played an integral part in the drafting of the first series of Geneva Conventions in 1864.

The Red Cross would continue to play an active role in the development and enforcement of the Geneva Conventions. New treaties, introducing controls on asphyxiating gases and expanding bullets came into force in 1899. Following the horrors of the First World War trenches, the Geneva Gas Protocol prohibited the use of poison gases and various forms of bacteriological warfare. In 1929 forty-seven Governments, including Great Britain, America, Russia, Germany and Japan signed two more Geneva Conventions dealing with the treatment of the wounded, and prisoners of war.

The Convention made it clear that prisoners of war must be treated humanely. Specifically, prisoners must not be subjected to torture or to medical or scientific experiments of any kind. They must be evacuated immediately from the combat zone, and be protected against violence, intimidation, insults and public curiosity. On no account could prisoners be used as human shields. Captors were allowed to question their prisoners, but this had to be conducted in the prisoner's native language and their response was entitled to be limited to name, rank, birth date and serial number. Prisoners refusing to answer any further questions must not be threatened or mistreated. During their period of captivity prisoners must be supplied with any medical treatment necessary, be kept reasonably warm and dry, and enjoy food rations equivalent to those serving in the captor's armed forces.

Despite the ideals of this Convention, the magnitude of World War Two made it impossible to police or enforce in any great measure.

The Red Cross conducted inspection visits, and censured miscreants whenever possible, but ultimately the humanitarian treatment of POWs was dictated by the nature of those in charge. The fate of those in captivity during the War became a lottery, dependant on where they were imprisoned and who were their captors.

Capture in battle is a traumatic experience. A common physical reaction to the immediate aftermath of combat, when the cacophony of engagement abruptly ceases and imminent danger is suddenly removed, is a period of shock. Being in enemy captivity also creates a sense of fear. Yet in many cases the trauma manifests itself in an overwhelming need to talk and share the recent experience. The natural sense of relief that the rigour of armed combat is over, when mixed with witnessing friends and colleagues being killed or wounded, also leads to crushing feelings of guilt. Many prisoners say that during this time they felt a profound need for comfort and support. Very often they will talk, unconditionally, to anyone that will listen, especially when their treatment by their captors is opposite to what they had expected. This is the period in which experienced interrogators can elicit vital information, without the need to contravene the Geneva Convention. At the start of the War, British Intelligence moved quickly to take full advantage of the expected influx of enemy prisoners from the planned offensive in France. Two men deemed to have the right credentials for the tasks were coaxed out of retirement.

When the patriotic Andrew Scotland arrived in South Africa in 1903 he was too late to join his brother in the British Army to fight against the Boers. Both Boer uprisings had been put down. Instead Scotland started work as a clerk for South Africa Territories Ltd and was dispatched to what is now Namibia. There his major client was the German Army, which at the time was engaged in a colonial war against the native Hottentot tribe.

Scotland decided that it would be beneficial to his career if he learnt to speak German. He also became friendly with the local Commandant, Hans von Quitzow. Impressed by the young Englishman, von Quitzow took the unusual step of offering him a commission in the German Army, with the challenging job of supervising supplies to men fighting in the bush. Scotland accepted and four years later was awarded the Order of the Red Eagle for his services.

Scotland's unusual role had not gone unnoticed by British Intelligence in Cape Town. On an appeal to his patriotism, Scotland agreed to supply information, mostly relating to the mentality prevailing within the German military, which was deemed increasing important as the two countries slid towards war in Europe. At the outbreak of the First World War, when this dual role became apparent to local German authorities, he was arrested and imprisoned.

Scotland was released after a year and on his return to Britain, in 1915, immediately volunteered to join the British Army. With his unusual background, and fluent German, he was dispatched for 'special duties' in France. His first job was to supervise the interrogation of German prisoners, specifically to obtain information about how their Army was able to return wounded soldiers back to the front more quickly than the British. Scotland's techniques involved a style of questioning that prisoners found unexpectedly friendly. His successful methods took full advantage of the emotional state of mind of the prisoner and by the end of the War, Scotland was in total charge of the processing of all enemy POWs.

On his return to civilian life he again worked within the German community, this time in South America. In 1933 Scotland, now in semi-retirement, took to touring Germany with his wife. By 1937 he was convinced that the Nazis would bring war to Europe. It was at this point that an old friend from South Africa set up a meeting between Scotland and Adolf Hitler. The Fuhrer was so impressed with the elderly Englishman that he invited him to join the newly formed Gestapo. Scotland declined.

When war broke out in 1939, Scotland was back in Britain, and resigned to the fact that, at sixty years of age, he was 'militarily unemployable'. He was wrong. By March 1940, Scotland, given the rank of Major, arrived in Arras, northern France, with the brief of establishing prisoner of war controls and interrogation structures to accommodate German captives expected when the Allies mounted their offensive. Events did not turn out as expected. When Major Scotland was evacuated in June, 40,000 Allied troops were in German captivity compared to the eighteen prisoners in his care.

When war broke out the internment of all German nationals residing in Britain became an immediate priority. The numbers were relatively small as traditionally few Germans had chosen to settle in Britain, and most of those in the country were Jewish refugees fleeing the Nazis. This was not the case with Italians. When Mussolini declared war on Britain on 10 June 1940 over 3,000 Italians, who had chosen Britain as their home, suddenly became 'undesirable aliens'.

Outside of London the largest community of Italians was in the coal mining valleys of south Wales. As long ago as the turn of the century a steady trickle of Italians, mostly hailing from the area around Bardi in the north of the country, established small cafes and ice-cream parlours in the bustling Welsh industrial towns. By the start of the War many had inter-married with locals and considered themselves as part of the community, and were treated in similar fashion.

When Italy joined the war, John Anderson, the minister in charge of national security (best remembered for his programme of building cheap metal air raid shelters bearing his name), immediately ordered that all 'B' Class Italian Aliens be interned. This was not meant to include men and women who had been resident for many years, many of whom were passionately opposed to the fascist regime in their native country. However, with feelings running high in the weeks after Dunkirk, Churchill stated that it was necessary to "collar the lot".

Overnight, police arrested all known Italians, even those married to British citizens, and interned them in a small number of camps established the previous year. In some cases entire Italian families were separated. The intention was to grade them into three categories. High-risk internees would be imprisoned for the duration of the war. Middle grades would be permitted to return home, with strict controls on their movements. Those assessed as low-grade security risks were to be allowed to return to their normal way of life.

Within days, conditions in the overcrowded camps become unbearable. Most internees were forced to sleep in tents, often without mattresses. Unsanitary conditions meant that disease quickly broke out. There were a number of incidents of suicide. The Home Office came up with a short term solution: the bulk of the internees would be deported to Canada, taking advantage of the fact that ships were constantly making that leg of the cross-Atlantic trip with empty holds. With stringent food rationing in Britain there was an additional benefit to any plan that reduced the numbers to be fed.

On 1 July 1940 the *Arandora Star*, a pre-war passenger liner, left Liverpool bound for Newfoundland. On board were 1,189 internees. At 7 o'clock, the following morning, the ship was 125 miles north-west of the coast of Ireland when she was attacked by a German U-Boat. Six hundred and sixty-one passengers and most of the crew were lost.

As the issue of immigrants was tackled, Major Scotland addressed that of military prisoners. The way he set about putting measures in place to accommodate and maximise intelligence opportunities presented by the capture of enemy personnel is indicative of the illogical optimism that pervaded senior British military. Convinced that the turning of the tide was only a matter of time, Scotland set up a system that still remains broadly similar to this day.

On 13 July 1940, less than a month after Dunkirk, the Prisoner of War Interrogation Service (Home) was established with Major Scotland in command. Although at this stage British troops had withdrawn from all fronts in Europe, Scotland was given twenty officers, with 'liberal transport', to set up regional centres around Britain where enemy personnel would be initially screened. These centres were immediately nicknamed 'cages'. Any prisoner deemed in possession of, or privy to, important information was transferred, for further interrogation, to a newly formed branch of Military Intelligence called MI19, headed by Major Norman Crockatt.

Crockatt had also seen distinguished service in the Great War, where he was badly wounded. Disillusioned with peacetime soldering, he had resigned his commission in 1927 but was enticed back in the months before World War Two by Major General Beaumont-Nesbitt, an old friend now the overall Director of Military Intelligence. Crockatt immediately accepted the offer and brought in his World War One deputy, Major A.W. Rawlinson, to take over operational command of what was now called the Combined Services Detailed Interrogation Centre. CSDIC was initially based, mostly for theatrical reasons, in the Tower of London, but with the onset of the Blitz was moved firstly to Cockfosters in north London and thereafter to the Buckinghamshire towns of Latimer and Beaconsfield.

For the three years following the British retreat from France, clients for both the Scotland's PWIS(H) and Crockatt's CSDIC were limited to Luftwaffe and Naval personnel captured after surviving crashes and sinkings. To house these prisoners after their initial integration a handful of POW Camps were opened, mostly in Scotland and the north of England. Guards for the camps tended to be selected from troops too old for front-line duty.

German officers were under the same obligation as their British counterparts to make every effort to escape and rejoin their country's war effort. The thousands of Allied troops being held in German camps on the European mainland did, however, enjoy two distinct advantages when attempting escape. First, their routes to neutral countries such as Switzerland and Spain were across land. Secondly, in

France, and Scandinavia, there were well-organised resistance movements in place to provide assistance. Escaping Germans, on the other hand, faced the problem of either having to cross the English Channel or North Sea in one direction, or the Irish Sea in the other. Escaping to Ireland did not provide any immediate return to action as the country, desperate to preserve its neutrality, operated an internment system for both Allied and German troops found on its shores. This led to the bizarre occurrence of warring sides sharing the same prison.

The geographical obstacle did not prevent a number of German escape attempts taking place during the early stages of the war. They were all unsuccessful, with one notable and spectacular exception. It is generally believed that the only German to repatriate himself from Allied captivity was Oberleutnant Franz von Werra, an ace fighter pilot who enjoyed a high profile in Germany prior to his capture. He had single-handedly destroyed seven British Hurricanes during the Battle of Britain and was awarded the Iron Cross. A further feat above the Thames estuary, "unique in the annals of fighter aviation", according to his citation, resulted in the Fuhrer personally presenting him with the Knight's Cross. The German media was full of the German hero posing with his pet lion, Simba.

Von Werra's initial tour of duty came to an end when his plane crashed while escorting a wave of Heinkel bombers en route to England. After being subjected to a particularly detailed interrogation by both PWIS(H) and CSDIC he was transferred to what was then the only POW camp in Britain, Grizedale Hall in the Lake District. There had been a number of unsuccessful attempts to escape from the camp prior to von Werra's arrival. Given the profile of the new prisoner, and fully aware of the propaganda opportunity his escape would present, the senior officers among the prisoners agreed that getting him back to Germany was a top priority. Being the first week of October 1940, time was of the essence to get him out before the approaching winter meant that any escape across the windswept terrain would be too hazardous.

A U-Boat commander, Kapitan-Leutnant Werner Lott, sold his watch and medals, through his batman, to British guards to provide von Werra with cash to aid his escape. Werra had the advantage of knowing the region following a pre-war walking holiday in the area. He chose to take advantage of the somewhat lax procedure of allowing the senior German officers to take a daily, albeit guarded, route march outside the camp to make his escape.

Knowing that the head count would not take place until the group returned to the camp, von Werra had already identified the point where he could drop over a small wall and make a dash to the nearby woods. Two local women saw him running away but the guards, out of earshot, did not notice their frantic handkerchief waving. By the time that the alarm was raised von Werra was already four miles away.

The resulting manhunt, carried out in the main by the police, Home Guard and local farmers, lasted for three days before von Werra was discovered in a farm building near Broughton Mills. His captors, two Home Guards, were escorting their captive to the Police Station when von Werra pushed the men down a steep bank and ran off into the descending dusk. He evaded further capture for three days before two local farmers saw him entering a stable and kept watch while police surrounded the building.

Von Werra was immediately transferred to a newly opened camp at Swanwick Hayes, a few miles north of Derby. He spent the first couple of weeks regaining his fitness with a strict routine of gymnastics and cold baths, before plotting a fresh escape with a handful of fellow Luftwaffe officers. This time the escape would be through a tunnel, which, by working around the clock, was completed in three weeks. On 21 December 1940, von Werra, along with four colleagues, broke out and, as agreed, made their separate ways. Within hours, von Werra was the only prisoner still at large. He was equipped with a forged identity card in the name of Captain Van Lott of the Royal Dutch Airforce, and a plan to find the nearest aerodrome and steal a plane to fly across the Channel. His method of finding an airfield was stunningly simple: he would ask.

As dawn was broke, von Werra, who spoke passable English with an accent that could plausibly be Dutch, knocked the door of a farmhouse and explained to the couple living there that his plane had crashed while returning from a mission over Denmark. Anxious to do what they could to help a brave pilot the farmer gave directions to the nearest railway station, while his wife made their guest a cup of tea. Von Werra thanked the couple for their hospitality and took his leave.

At the nearby Codner Park station, von Werra explained his supposed plight to the booking clerk who telephoned the nearest R.A.F. base at Hucknall and passed on the 'Dutch' airman's request for transport to collect him. The clerk was obviously not totally convinced by Werra's story and took the precaution of alerting the police. When two local constables arrived, aware of the escape that night from Swanwick Hayes, they began a line of questioning aimed to trip up the stranded pilot. Von Werra was more than prepared. He was armed with a copy of the previous day's *Times*, along with a supply of English cigarettes, and assumed the policemen were aware that he was not allowed to carry anything other than his basic ID in case he was captured behind enemy lines. The officers were convinced that the pilot was genuine and while waiting for von Werra's lift to arrive, listened to his stories about previous bombing missions against the hated Nazis that had occupied his homeland.

On arriving at the R.A.F. camp, von Werra was greeted by the duty officer who asked him where his squadron was based. Again he was well prepared. He told the British officer that his home aerodrome was Dyce, Aberdeen. Von Werra knew that a phone call would be made, but banked on connections being slow to the north of Scotland. He was right. As attempts were made to connect with R.A.F. Dyce, von Werra quietly left the duty office and made for the planes parked alongside the runway. After demonstrating the controls of the Hurricane that von Werra had chosen to make the final leg of his journey, an obliging mechanic went to get the trolley-accumulator needed to start the engine. But by now von Werra's luck had run out and the next voice he heard was the aggrieved duty officer who was pointing a gun into the German's neck.

A few months later the duty officer received a postcard from America with a cheeky greeting in von Werra's handwriting: he had been sent to a camp in Canada. From here his third attempt to escape was successful and he crossed the St. Lawrence River aboard a goods train into the United States, still a neutral country. The American authorities were in a quandary as to what to do with the escapee, eventually deciding on a temporary compromise whereby the German Embassy posted bail of $15,000. Not surprisingly, von Werra skipped the country and eventually returned home to Germany via Mexico, Peru and Brazil. He was given a hero's welcome on his arrival and assumed command of a Luftwaffe squadron. In August 1941 his Messerschmitt crashed into the sea off the coast of Holland. His body was never found.

7. TURNING TIDES

By the new year of 1941 Hitler had abandoned hope of both a negotiated peace with, or an invasion of, Britain. While the threat of an invasion remained, the new strategy was to deprive the British Isles of all vital supplies and starve the country into submission. Hitler had already made the decision that would lose the war: Germany was to invade Russia.

Although the Fuhrer dismissed the reservations of his Generals in respect of Russia, he did agree with their advice that before the invasion could commence the Balkans needed to be secured. Bulgaria and Romania had committed themselves to pacts with the Nazis. The problems lay with Greece and Yugoslavia. Against Hitler's wishes, Mussolini, not satisfied with the Italian occupation of Albania, had invaded neighbouring Greece in October 1940. The invasion was an abject failure. Within a month the Greek Army, with assistance from Britain, had driven the Italian troops back practically to the border, where a stalemate prevailed into the following spring. To add to Hitler's problem in the region, on 27 March a military coup in Yugoslavia had overthrown the government that had previously entered into a pact with him.

Hitler dispatched his two favoured Generals: Von Rundstedt was to assume overall command, with Generalfeldmarschall Ewald von Kleist in command of the armoured forces. In the meantime, Italy suffered another embarrassing defeat in North Africa where British troops, although greatly outnumbered, forced the Italian Army to retreat westwards out of Egypt. Churchill, flushed with this success, immediately dispatched much of this victorious Army to assist in the defence of Greece. Although the combined British, Greek and Yugoslav forces were no match for the resources at von Rundstedt's disposal, they succeeded in delaying the German advance until May, when a mini version of Dunkirk was required to evacuate the Allied troops first to Crete, and then back to North Africa.

It was the delay in securing the Balkans that would directly lead to Germany's failure to defeat Russia. To avoid the same fate as Napoleon, 130 years before, the Third Reich needed to capture Moscow before the onset of the savage weather. With spring, and half the summer already gone, Hitler's advisors urged him to at least postpone the invasion of Russia for nine months and concentrate instead on the eastern Mediterranean islands of Cyprus and Malta, which would provide the platform to seize the Suez Canal and then the oilfields of the Middle East. Hitler refused and ordered the invasion of Russia to commence on 22 June 1941. History would show that the order was a month too late.

Three German Army groups were to be used. The northern one, under Generalfeldmarschall Emil Leeb was to advance from East Prussia, through the Baltic states towards Leningrad. The central Army, commanded by Generalfeldmarschall Bock, was to strike from Warsaw, with Moscow as their goal. Von Rundstedt was to take charge of the southern Army, their immediate target being Kiev. All objectives needed to be met before the onset of the dreaded Russian winter.

Within days it became apparent that the Generals had been right. This would not be a repeat of the *Blitzkrieg* through the Low Countries and France. For one thing the vastness of Russia did not enjoy the benefit of anything resembling western European roads. Secondly, Russian troops, and the people, were prepared to fight to the death to defend their country. The weather intervened sooner than expected, with unseasonal rain during early July reducing the dirt tracks to quagmires.

The northern Army made the best progress and by late September the city of Leningrad was under siege. The middle Army were suffering the worst of the conditions, and a decision was made to divert the bulk of these forces southwards to assist von Rundstedt's troops, which were on the verge of seizing Kiev. The city was occupied on 19 September and a month later southern Russia, as far east as Rostov-on-Don, was under German occupation. The priority now shifted back to a final push towards Moscow but the first heavy snows fell on 25 October. Von Rundstedt urged that the offensive should be broken off and a suitable winter line be taken. Once more, Hitler dismissed the advice out of hand, this time with the support of both Bock and Generalfeldmarschall von Brauchitsch, the Fuhrer's favoured military advisor at High Command. By late November it looked as if those advocating the continuing advance were to be proved right. With 11,000 citizens of Leningrad already dead, many as a result of starvation, the city could not possibly hold out much longer. Further south Moscow was almost within striking distance.

The Russians had deliberately waited until the depth of winter to launch their counter-offensive. With 85,000 German troops already dead, and the survivors experiencing conditions they could not have envisaged in their worse nightmares, Russia struck back. As the Leningrad Radio Symphony Orchestra defiantly broadcast a performance of Beethoven's 9th to the B.B.C. in London, to the south of the country German troops were being forced out of Rostov. By the end of the second week of December the German front line had got as near to the capital as they would get, and had now been pushed 50 miles west of Moscow. For the first time in the war, the Army of the Third Reich was in retreat.

In North Africa the year had witnessed another war of attrition. Hitler had dispatched one of his rising military stars, General Erwin Rommel, to shore up the mess caused by Italian capitulation. Churchill, desperate for a moral boosting victory, ignored advice to strengthen the British garrison in Singapore against the growing threat from Japan and sent as much military resource as he could to push for outright control of the desert. Rommel, using bold new tactics, drove the British eastwards for six months before they counter attacked, both sides ending the year in roughly the same position that they had started from. As if sharing the fate of Napoleon in Russia and the setback in North Africa was not bad enough for Hitler, his Axis partners in the Far East were in the process of executing an attack that would change the face of the War.

Japan had made its expansionist aims clear ten years previously with the invasion of the Chinese province of Manchuria. When France fell to Germany and the Vichy Government was established, Japan, with the support of its Axis partners proceeded with a 'protected' occupation of French Indo-China. The neutral American Government considered this more of a threat than events in Europe, and when Japan refused his demand to withdraw, President Roosevelt froze all Japanese assets in America and placed an embargo on oil supply. Churchill, spotting a long-awaited opportunity to force America off the fence, immediately followed suit. Japan, with no oil of her own, was forced into a corner.

The Japanese response was to enter into intense diplomatic negotiation, while simultaneously planning a military offensive of staggering proportion. At five to eight on the morning of 7 December 1941, Japan attacked, and virtually destroyed, the American Pacific Fleet moored at its base at Pearl Harbour in Hawaii. Simultaneously Japanese troops commenced the invasion of Hong Kong, the

Philippines, and Malaya, from where they proceeded north towards British-held Burma and south towards Singapore. The Philippines, with strong support from America would hold out for six months. The British outpost of Hong Kong had fallen by Christmas. Rangoon, Mandalay and the Burma Road to China were under Japanese occupation by the following April. Worst of all for Britain was the fall of the naval stronghold at Singapore. If a date can be determined when the sun set on the British Empire, it was Sunday 15 February 1942. The tide of the war, however, would turn in 1942, and each of the main theatres saw pivotal battles. In Russia it was Stalingrad; in North Africa it was El Alamein, and in the Pacific, the naval battle at Midway.

On 5 January 1942, a German convoy reached the North African port of Tripoli with the fresh batch of tanks that Rommel had been demanding for some months. With them he quickly launched an eastern offensive towards British-held Egypt. Six months later he wrote to his wife, "Only 100 more miles to Alexandria!" By the end of the following day the crucial port was within sixty miles and the British fleet were fleeing through the nearby Suez Canal, south to the Red Sea. All that remained between Rommel and his goal was the salt and soft sand surrounding the town of El Alamein. With the summer heat at its fiercest, and with intelligence that overstated the extent of the remaining British resistance, Rommel paused. Crucially, this allowed the Allied forces to regroup and a quirk of fate to intervene.

Churchill had decided to give command of the 8th Army in North Africa to Lieutenant General Gott, but when he was killed in a plane crash en route to Cairo he was replaced by General Bernard Montgomery. The confrontation at El Alamein consisted of several battles, which were already under way when the new Commander took charge. The crucial encounters took place between 31 August to 3 September, when the 'Desert Rats' not only stopped the advancing German and Italian troops, but succeeded in forcing a retreat. It was as far east as Rommel would get.

A jubilant Churchill, his position under extreme political pressure by now, hailed the victory long and loud. Planning to use the success at El Alamein as the springboard for a fresh campaign with his new found American allies, the British Prime Minister urged his star commander to press on and run the Axis Army westwards. Montgomery resisted, determined to wait until preparations for an offensive were ready. The first British advance finally began on 23

October. Twice Rommel's Army held its line. The third time it gave way and Rommel requested an order from Hitler to instigate a structured retreat. Any of his fellow officers in Russia would have told Rommel this was a forlorn hope. What resulted was pointless resistance, and an unnecessary loss of life and tanks. By early November, the Axis troops were back to the position they had started the year from, and Churchill, champing at the bit, could go ahead with Operation Torch, an Allied invasion of north west Africa.

By the end of April 1942, much of the American fleet had been rebuilt, and national pride marginally restored by a daring bombing raid on Tokyo. On 3 May the American Navy won the crucial Battle of Coral Sea, which prevented the Japanese occupation of New Guinea extending to the southern town of Port Moresby, dangerously close to the northern coast of Australia. The Japanese response was to engineer a major naval battle in which it intended to wipe out the resurgent American fleet at the remote, but strategically vital, Pacific island of Midway.

Early bombardment of American positions achieved the objective of drawing American ships into the area. The Japanese sensed victory after 35 of the 41 planes American planes launched from their carriers were destroyed. However, a fresh wave of 37 dive-bombers, launched from the *USS Enterprise*, caught the Japanese Navy by surprise. All four of their carriers were sunk. America had regained control of the Pacific and Allied troops began slowly, and bloodily, reversing Japanese advances on land.

After being overruled by Hitler in respect of a retreat in Russia during the onset of the winter of 1941, and now in ill health, von Rundstedt resigned his command. When the failure of the campaign became apparent to the rest of the world, Walter von Brauchitsch was made the scapegoat, and Hitler assumed direct command of the entire German Army. He proceeded to replace Leeb, who had backed von Rundstedt, and gave responsibility for the main spring offensive in the south to von Manstein. The immediate target was the Black Sea port of Sebastopol, then west to Stalingrad, which would lead to an objective more important than Moscow: the Caucasus oilfields. Although Leningrad had, against all odds, survived the winter it seemed only a matter of time before the city surrendered. Even Hitler had to accept that the best the middle Army could hope for was to resist a further Russian advance. If Stalingrad could be taken then a fresh attack could be made on Moscow from the south.

By the onset of the second winter of the campaign, the citizens of Leningrad still proudly stood up to their siege and Russian troops, now enjoying regular supplies of equipment from both Britain and America, had pushed the middle German Army to a front 200 miles from Moscow. Von Manstein, however, had enjoyed success, albeit slow, in the south. In early November the German frontline was engaged in street fighting on the outskirts of Stalingrad. The Russians, knowing the local weather and terrain, chose their moment to strike back. The counter-attack launched on 19 and 20 of November took advantage of a brief interval between the first strong frosts of winter and the forthcoming heavy snows, which clog all motorised movement. On frost hardened firm ground, Russian troops struck with ferocity, catching their enemy in a trough of exhaustion. Within days it was the Axis Army that was in a state of siege. A quarter of a million German, Italian and Romanian soldiers were trapped by a pincer movement on the outskirts of Stalingrad. Hitler's refusal to allow their surrender had an element of ruthless logic: it allowed von Manstein to regroup for another spring offensive.

Yet 1943 saw a further gradual erosion of Hitler's eastern ambition. Von Manstein launched an offensive from Kursk in July, but the campaign was resisted and, with the Russia Army now moving forward, by the end of the year Kiev, 400 miles to the west, was again under Russian control. In the field of military strategy the ability to conduct an orderly retreat is often a greater achievement than commanding an advance. Von Kleist was promoted to the rank of Generalfeldmarschall for his efforts in taking charge of the retreat across the Sea of Azov into the Crimea. However, by the beginning of the German Army's third Russian winter, Hitler was again issuing the order that "every man must fight where he stands".

It would take another two and a half years for Russian troops to enter Berlin. Four million Axis troops and over eight million Russian troops would lose their lives in the campaign. Leningrad would hold out for a total of 880 days during which 641,000 civilians would die. In total seventeen million Russian civilians were killed during the war, some as a result of Nazi atrocities.

Germany's attempts to starve Britain of food and arms would also fail, but not until a four year battle to control the supply routes had been fought out in the Atlantic and Arctic oceans. With German planes able to attack shipping far out to the west from their new bases in Norway and France, and with Ireland grimly hanging on to its neutral status and refusing Allied shipping access to its ports, by 1940 the British people were enduring severe rationing, especially of food and petrol.

Germany's advantage at sea lay in the U-Boats. However Britain enjoyed superior intelligence in intercepting coded messages of naval movements. A deadly game of cat and mouse ensued with 'Wolfpacks' of U-Boats hunting the vulnerable convoys constantly in transit between North America, Europe and Russia. Millions of tons of military and commercial ships were lost. Tens of thousands of Royal and Merchant Naval personnel drowned. But very slowly the Allies gained the upper hand.

At the start of 1942 Hitler correctly surmised that Churchill planned to invade Norway and transferred many of the Luftwaffe bombers attacking Allied convoys to defence duties. Churchill had been talked out of the invasion, but Hitler's response shifted the balance in the Atlantic marginally towards the Allies. By the summer the odds moved back towards Germany with the launch of a new class of U-Boat. The sinking of five Brazilian ships in August led to a declaration of war by Brazil which allowed Allied shipping to use its ports – a significant advantage in the southern ocean.

America was deeply involved in the War, and events around the world were beginning to swing towards the Allies. However, Britain was still only receiving a third of its pre-war imports, and Churchill's increasing desire to invade Europe could not be accommodated until the battle for the North Atlantic was won.

Early 1943 changes in naval command for both sides took place. Admiral Raeder had fallen out with Hitler, while Churchill had appointed Admiral Max Horton. Horton, with new anti-submarine equipment at his disposal, went on the offensive against the U-Boat fleet. By May U-Boat losses had doubled from the previous month. Two months later, for the first time since the outbreak of war, more Allied ships were being launched than were being sunk. By the mid-summer of 1943 German naval and air presence in the North Atlantic was minimal and the supply lines were at last clear for the much-anticipated invasion of Europe.

With Operation Torch successfully completed the previous November, the Allies developed an invasion strategy using Sicily as the entry point to Europe. On 9 July 1943 250,000 British, and 228,000 American troops, more than would be employed the following year in Normandy, landed on European soil. Within a month,

Mussolini had been imprisoned after a military coup. Hitler antici-pated that Italy would sue for peace and prepared German troops to turn on its ally. He was correct. On 3 September, as Allied troops were crossing the Straits of Messina into mainland Italy, the country signed an armistice agreement. The German Army surged south as the Allies moved north. Four months of fierce fighting would eventually result in a line being drawn 100 miles south of Rome. German airborne troops had sprung Mussolini from prison and he proceeded to set up a fascist regime in German-occupied northern Italy.

In the meantime, tens of thousands of American troops were trav-elling across the Atlantic to a temporary home in Britain, as they prepared for a full-scale invasion of Northern France, codenamed Operation Overlord, to take place on a date still to be decided – D-Day.

8. SPECIAL RELATIONSHIPS

The arrival of American troops gave Britain a much-needed boost. US soldiers had been fighting alongside their British allies for over a year, in North Africa, Italy and the Far East, but this was the first time, for most people, that they had seen an American soldier in the flesh. Compared to bedraggled and battered British troops, the Americans were well-groomed, well-dressed and well-fed. Nobody on the home front begrudged American involvement, some merely believed that it should have happened sooner.

President Roosevelt's clear statement of neutrality, delivered within days of the outbreak of war, and only a few hours after twenty-eight Americans civilians had perished in the U-Boat attack on the British passenger liner *Athenia*, set the tone for the first year. The American public had no stomach for another conflict; memories of the carnage of the Great War were still vivid. Hitler was a problem for Europe to deal with.

Chamberlain had immediately exerted pressure on the President and despite his public stance, Roosevelt moved quickly to provide practical assistance to Britain. On 3 November 1939 he persuaded Congress to amend the American Neutrality Act, which prevented the shipment of American arms to belligerent countries. The changes made Germany the aggressor, Britain and France its victims.

Roosevelt's hopes for being able to broker an early peace were dashed when his envoy, Sumner Welles, returned empty handed from a whirlwind diplomacy mission to Berlin, Rome, Paris and London. His task was not helped by Britain making a raid on German iron ore in Norway hours before he arrived in the British capital.

When Churchill became Prime Minister, his strength of character, and inspirational oratory increased the pressure on Roosevelt. A regular exchange of telegrams between the men began, a method of communication that would continue until the final weeks of the war. Churchill's messages alternated between unashamed begging and blatant appeals to guilt. Roosevelt remained unmoved.

Even after France had fallen, and continued British resistance looked impossible, Roosevelt had no intention of being directly involved in the widening conflict. Neither the Senate or Congress wanted war, and Roosevelt was close enough to public opinion to know that the majority of his public supported this position. Both were important factors in the run-up to a presidential election. America was, however, beginning to sense a danger from Japan. As the Battle of Britain raged, Roosevelt passed an act authorising the American Pacific fleet be doubled in size.

Within forty-eight hours of being re-elected in November 1940, the President was confident enough in his position to increase direct, and practical, help to Britain. Although he still had no intention of committing American troops, Roosevelt promised seventy reconditioned troop ships and three hundred new merchant vessels. He also had devised an ingenious way for Britain to pay for them. With British gold reserves now almost depleted, 'Lend-Lease', effectively a take-now-pay-whenever-you-can arrangement, was put into place. Using one of his famous fireside radio chats to go public on the help, he labelled America the 'great arsenal of democracy'.

Two months later America began making food supplies to Britain. King George broadcast his personal thanks. The following November, Presidential pressure forced the US Congress to vote, by 212 votes to 194, in favour of allowing merchant ships into British waters. The extent of opposition for what remained indirect help was a clear indication that America was still a long way from a military commitment. Three weeks later Pearl Harbour was attacked.

It is a popular misconception that the Japanese attack brought America to Britain's aid. From the moment the first bomb landed, America was at war with Japan, which made America's entry into the European war even more unlikely. Roosevelt would never have got his Government to sanction two wars at once. However, four days after Pearl Harbour, Hitler made perhaps his biggest single mistake in declaring war on America. Quite what the thinking behind this course of action was is not clear. Nonetheless, from that defining moment, the question of American entry into the European conflict was academic.

Churchill wasted no time. Within three weeks he met Roosevelt in Washington to establish an Anglo-American General Staff charged with co-ordinating strategies against the Axis of Germany, Italy and Japan. Stalin was soon invited to make a triumvirate of opposition, and Churchill was already talking of an Allied invasion of Western Europe. But two years later, Churchill was waiting impatiently. As American troops poured into Britain in autumn 1943, argument was raging amongst the Allied leaders as to timing. There would be only one chance to get it right. The eventual day may have been eight months away, but there would be no question that the American troops stationed in Britain would not be fully prepared.

★

The roots of the US 28th Infantry Division can be traced back to 1747, when Benjamin Franklin formed his battalion of 'Associators' in Philadelphia. Other units were quickly formed in Pennsylvania during the American Revolution. A hundred years later, in 1878, Governor John F. Hartranft formed a single National Guard for the State and appointed himself as Commanding Officer of the 28th. The Division fought alongside the British for the first time during the final months of the Great War. From May to November 1918, the 28th suffered 16,000 battle casualties. At the end of the War, in acknowledgement of their services, the Division was allowed to wear the Red Keystone, symbol of Pennsylvania, on their uniform and became affectionately known as 'The Keystones'.

Along with other National Guards, the 28th was activated in February 1941 and dispatched to the coasts of Louisiana and Florida to train in amphibious warfare. The Division was not called to front line service when war broke out in the Pacific, nor did it join American troops in North Africa. The 28th was being kept back for the Western European campaign. Mountain manoeuvres in West Virginia preceded the Division being dispatched across the Atlantic on October 8 1943. Ten days later, led by Major General Lloyd D. Brown, it arrived safely in south Wales, home for the next six months.

The Division set up its headquarters in the mock gothic castle at Margam Park, near to the steelworks town of Port Talbot. Colonel William Blanton, commander of the largest regiment, the 109th Infantry, was also based there. His men set up camps along the coast. In line with rest of the American Army, the Keystones were segregated; black soldiers were placed in tented billets near to the sand dunes of Merthyr Mawr, five miles south of Bridgend. There was an ideal, purpose built, location for the men of the 2nd Battalion, led by Major Neri Cangelosi. The dormitory accommodation built at Island Farm for the munitions workers had largely been unused. The entire 28th Division, which would be one of the most highly decorated units in the Allied forces, was billeted at Island Farm.

Straight away, there was an affinity between the Americans and their Welsh hosts. Maintaining morale was a top priority. These soldiers knew that they going to the front line, but not even their commanders knew when. It could be within weeks, or not until well into the following year. Interminable waiting can have a debilitating effect on a soldier. There would be time to get these troops as well trained and prepared as possible, but they also needed to have their minds diverted.

Fraternisation was actively encouraged, and among the young ladies of South Wales the glamorous Yanks were more than welcomed to Saturday night dances in Bridgend and Porthcawl. American officers became regulars in the local pubs. Many of the troops were keen sportsmen, some verging on professional standard prior to America going to war. They would not be around when that most baffling of British sports, cricket, started its season in the spring, but football and rugby were there to occupy them on their arrival. To Americans rugby is the closest sport to their version of football. It was not long before American commanders decided to demonstrate their winter game to the Welsh.

Two exhibition matches were arranged, at Swansea's St Helen's ground and at the Brewery Field, home of Bridgend Rugby Club. Billed as 'Armoured Rugger', the matches pitted together rivals who were easily as bitter as any traditional adversaries in Wales. The 'Screaming Eagles' of the elite 101st Airborne Paratroop Division were to play the 'Keystone Invaders.' The Keystones took to the field in blue, while the Screaming Eagles sported gaudy green shorts and shirts, adorned by flaming yellow helmets. The headgear bemused the Welsh crowd, who questioned why such protection was needed. They soon found out. No quarter was asked, or given, and American commanders must have feared as the casualties mounted. The umpire, Lieutenant Edward Sauer, suffered the worst injury. When he broke his leg it provided training under battle conditions for the local Red Cross as their ambulance sped across the field to the stricken soldier. The matches were drawn and the *Western Mail*'s rugby correspondent shared the bewilderment of the non-American portion of the large crowd. American rugger was "an acquired taste". Too many "spurts and stops do not lend themselves to speed and endeavour."

A sport, identical on both sides of the Atlantic, also provided competitive recreation for the Americans when they took on the marksmen of the South Wales Home Guard. A number of shooting tournaments took place, prompting the commander of the Home Guard to write to his opposite number at Margam Park. Colonel Llewelyn wrote: "I have greatly appreciated the contacts I have been able to make with your officers and men since you have been here, and I feel that in this way our two nations can discover how very closely linked we are in our general outlook, the friendships now being made will be lasting, for therein lies the only hope for the future of the World. Probably more good has been done yesterday than by all the hot air belched forth by our respective national propaganda machines!"

As the penultimate Christmas of the war approached, the American troops decided to thank their guests, who had endured years of strict rationing. Lavish Christmas lunches, topped off with gifts, were laid on for children across south Wales, particular attention being given to evacuees, many of whom had been orphaned during the Blitz.

Most of the troops' time was spent in training exercises. Everyone knew that at some future time they would be landing on a heavily fortified continental beach. The coastlines of south Wales, and north Devon, visible across the Bristol Channel, were very similar to northern France. The 109th spent long days practicing manoeuvres, both on the Gower Peninsula and across the channel in Woolacombe. Days that the sea was particularly choppy were favoured, in order to get the men most prone to seasickness used to the worst possible conditions.

One major exercise was 'The Hedgehog' whereby entire rifle battalions attacked a network of pillboxes, supported by overhead artillery, mortars, tanks and air bombardment. The most gruelling exercise was a hundred-mile hike over the Brecon Beacons. The Allied commanders were relaxed that German intelligence would be reporting each move. In a way, the exercises were viewed as a demonstration of strength. Both sides knew the invasion was coming. The mystery remained as to where and when it would occur.

The whole of south Wales was buzzing with activity directed at what everyone hoped would signal the final phase of the War. Shipyards worked around the clock armouring hundreds of merchant vessels commandeered for the invasion. A strange concrete construction appeared off the coast of Porthcawl. It would eventually be towed to France and form the basis of the floating Mulberry Harbour, capable of handling the large number of troop carriers that would soon be spewing their human cargoes onto the European mainland.

Despite Churchill's impatience, the first time that an Allied invasion of Western Europe was discussed at the highest level took place when the British Prime Minister visited the home of the American President on 19 August 1943. The third ally, Stalin, was not present, but he had made his position known. The sooner that a third front could be opened in Europe, adding to his campaign in the east, and the recent Allied landings in Sicily, the sooner the war would be over. Churchill was swayed by the American argument that caution was needed, but dismissed the notion that Berlin could be reached through Italy, and consequently an extra campaign was not required. A target date of 1 May 1944 was set for Operation Overlord, the invasion of northern France. There was one other major item on the agenda. It resulted in an agreement for scientists from Britain and the U.S. to collaborate on the production of an atomic bomb.

The next decision addressed the appointment of the leader with overall military control of Overlord. Of all the candidates, the one with the least combat experience was chosen. Dwight D. Eisenhower had not experienced an active command before taking over the responsibility for the American landings in North Africa the year before. A brilliant graduate from West Point in 1915, Eisenhower had been spared the traumas of Europe during the Great War. His career up until Pearl Harbour had been impressive, but confined to administrative roles. The onset of war for America catapulted him to a senior military post in the White House, where the President noticed his organisational and diplomatic talents.

Eisenhower's appointment as Commander of the Allied African troops had been controversial. He was commanding high profile Generals such as George Patton, under whom he had once served. For the appointment of commander for the invasion of Sicily, Eisenhower was first choice over the British candidate, Bernard Montgomery. As Churchill and Roosevelt made their monumental plans, Eisenhower was three weeks away from progressing the Allied Mediterranean invasion from Sicily. By the time his appointment to Overlord was announced the Allied forces were in stalemate, halfway up the Italian mainland.

The man who would later become the 34th President of the United States possessed two overwhelming talents. One was the skill of planning on a massive scale; the other was the ability to retain popularity down the line, while being more than able to manage the inflated egos around and above him. When he arrived in London to take up his appointment as Supreme Commander of the Allied Expeditionary Forces he found himself in day-to-day contact with Winston Churchill. It did not faze him.

Plans were still on track for an invasion on 1 May. The German defence forces were commanded by General von Rundstedt, who Hitler had brought out of retirement and who was held in the highest regard by Eisenhower and the Allied top brass. Von Rundstedt's very presence engendered an even greater level of caution. Nothing was to be left to chance. As British and American troops maintained a state of readiness, a bizarre intelligence leak towards the end of March delayed the invasion. A package containing documents outlining critical details of Overlord were intercepted by the US Post in an area of Chicago heavily populated by US citizens of German extraction. The culprit turned out to be a low ranking soldier, who when asked to forward the package had inadvertently written the address of his sick sister instead of the War Department in Washington. His excuse was believed, but before the sensitivity of the documents had been realised in Chicago, four unauthorised Army personnel and at least ten postal workers had seen them. At Eisenhower's office, plans needed to be re-made.

D-Day, as the landings were now called, was put back until 31 May. A frustrated Eisenhower took the opportunity to make a whistle stop tour of American troops. On 1 April he met with senior officers at the Seabank Hotel in Porthcawl to update them of the invasion plans. He went on to nearby Margam Castle to address junior officers and selected lower ranks of the 28th Army. Standing in the grounds, Eisenhower, a polished public speaker, galvanised the troops. His motorcade left Margam to make the long journey back to London. Ten miles up the road Eisenhower directed his driver to make a detour to Island Farm. Here, to a group of cheering troops he repeated his speech, standing on the back of a Jeep.

Ten days later the 28th Army moved out of Wales to their next temporary home in Wiltshire. They were about to serve an unprecedented 196 combat days in Europe, almost every one of them spent in fierce action. They left a strong bond with the local communities which remains sixty years later. It is estimated that 350 marriages occurred as a result of the six months the Americans spent in south Wales.

9. D-DAY

By the spring of 1944 even its formidable propaganda machine could not hide the fact that the war had turned against Germany. The Allies controlled North Africa and were making slow, costly progress north through Italy. To the east, the Russian Red Army was moving steadily towards Poland. The remaining Axis partner, Japan, was also broadly in retreat throughout the Far East. Hitler knew that an Allied landing in Western Europe was now only a matter of time, but retained an unwavering belief that the Third Reich would emerge victorious. His confidence was based on the development of a range of 'super weapons'.

As early as 1937 Hitler had instigated a programme of rocket development at a top-secret location, Peenemunde, on the Baltic coast. Two renowned scientists, Dr. Walter Dornberger and Dr. Werner von Braun were the key members of a team whose work would, ironically, be the foundation of America's post-war space programme. The project was given the name *Vergeltungswaffe* — 'vengeance weapon'. Two distinct types of machine were to be developed. The first, called V1, was a form of jet propelled, unmanned, aeroplane capable of carrying a bomb load in excess of 2,000 pounds. The second, the V2, was much more ambitious. The machine was, at inception, a figment of science fiction: a rocket capable of reaching the limits of the earth's atmosphere before falling back to Earth armed with an explosive cargo. On 3 October 1942, the V1 made its inaugural flight. It went into production at S.S.-run factories, manned by slave labour. Under increasing pressure from Hitler, his team of military scientists and S.S. factory managers reported that the first V1 rockets would be ready to attack Britain by the middle of June 1944.

Back in the conventional military world the threat of an Allied invasion of Western Europe loomed. Less than four months after he had willingly accepted his resignation in Russia, Hitler reinstated the veteran Field Marshal Gerd von Rundstedt to the command of the Western Army. For von Rundstedt it was an unusual and frustrating role. Plans to invade Britain had been aborted and he spent the first two years of his posting watching America enter the war and the Allies prepare for the invasion of Europe. His primary task was to supervise the construction of vast concrete defences and minefields along the coast from Holland to the Atlantic border between France and Spain.

As the Allied build-up to invasion gathered momentum during the first half of 1944, Generals von Rundstedt and Eisenhower played out an elaborate game of chess. Von Rundstedt was convinced that the Allies would invade across the shortest stretch of water, landing somewhere between Calais and Boulogne. After all, this was the cross-channel route recommended to make the journey in the opposite direction four years ago. Hitler was not convinced. His judgment was that the landings would occur on the stretch of Normandy coastline as near as possible to the strategically important river port of Caen. Field-Marshal Rommel, who was now von Rundstedt's second-in-command, gradually came round to the Fuhrer's train of thought. Hitler's logic was backed up by intelligence in March that Allied troops had conducted a massive training exercise in North Devon on beaches very similar to those in Normandy.

Von Rundstedt and Rommel also disagreed as to how the invasion should be repelled. Rommel favoured defeating the invading Army as soon as they landed. Von Rundstedt argued that as they did not know for certain where the invasion would take place, then the form of defence that provided the most flexibility was to position the bulk of German tank forces inland, moving them towards the enemy as soon as it was clear where the landing was going to take place. As this would not be known until the troop carriers were less than two hours away from their destinations, the plan called for impeccable communication and a state of constant readiness.

Throughout May 1944, German reconnaissance planes confirmed that a massive concentration of Allied troops was taking place along the southern coast of England that could be deployed in a direction that took them towards anywhere between Calais and Cherbourg. The other unknown was when the invasion was to take place. Von Rundstedt was adamant that Eisenhower could not move until he was guaranteed at least four consecutive days of good weather. On 1 June, when the German Commander-in-Chief received his weather report forecasting unsettled conditions for the following week, he sent a communication to Hitler stating that there was no prospect of an Allied invasion for at least another five days. Rommel, still smarting at von Rundstedt's dismissal of his request for a second Panzer Division to be moved in to the area surrounding Caen, took advantage of the brief respite to visit Hitler at his headquarters in East Prussia to argue his case in person.

Throughout the War, British Intelligence had been highly successful in the interception of coded messages between the German military. During the dark days of 1940 and 1941 it was practically the only advantage Britain enjoyed. The 6,000-strong team at Bletchley Park quickly deciphered von Rundstedt's latest message to Hitler and immediately passed it to Eisenhower. The Allied Commander had formed the same conclusion as his German counterpart in respect of the weather and D-Day was already postponed until conditions improved. Now knowing von Rundstedt's thoughts, Eisenhower weighed up the disadvantage that the elements would cause to the operation against the benefit of surprise, a great military advantage, and gave the order for the invasion to commence.

At five minutes to midnight on June 5, members of the British 6th Airborne Division landed by glider, six miles north of Caen and proceeded to cut German communication lines. The first wave of troop ships had already left port and by dawn American soldiers were landing on the first of five Normandy beaches.

Despite von Rundstedt's title of Commander-in-Chief, Hitler retained total control of his Army. Anything above and beyond minor troop movements needed the personal sanction of the Fuhrer himself. On hearing the news that the Allied landings were underway, and where they were heading, von Rundstedt immediately telephoned German High Command to obtain permission to move his reserve divisions towards Normandy. Von Rundstedt tended to avoid speaking to Hitler, if at all possible, and made his request to General Alfred Jodl, Chief of Operations at High Command, and waited for permission. Most military historians agree that the extraordinary course of action that Jodl took had a profound effect on the success of the landing. He decided not to disturb Hitler's sleep and took it upon himself to refuse von Rundstedt's request, believing the approaching Allied ships were a decoy. Rommel received news of the invasion while travelling to Prussia and immediately returned to his command post on the evening of June 6th. Had Rommel been at his desk when the invasion became apparent it is likely that, given his relationship with Hitler, he would have spoken directly to the Fuhrer.

Twelve hours after landing on the beaches, and despite suffering heavy losses, the Allied Army had established a crucial foothold. Eisenhower's original objective was to take Caen within days but it became quickly apparent that this would be impossible. It took four days to build the crucial artificial Mulberry Harbour, allowing the 150,000 troops that had made the first landings to be doubled. By now the German reinforcements had arrived, but slowly the Allied Army moved inland, claiming Cherbourg on 29 June. Hitler's reaction was to sack von Rundstedt.

★

On June 13, people in Bethnal Green, east London, hardened by almost four years of German bombing, but heartened by news of the much awaited invasion of France, saw a strange object in the sky. A small aircraft, around twenty-five feet long, without any form of propeller, was travelling low and emitting a loud buzzing noise. As the engine suddenly cut out the plane plummeted to the ground, detonating a ton of explosive on impact and killing six people.

They were not to know that the inventors of this deadly new weapon, Doctors Dornberger and Braun, had spent a frustrating morning at the launch site at Watten on the Channel coast. The first five rockets had crashed on take-off. The next went down in the sea. More refinements were made but news filtering back that the next three had reached the English coast but fallen far short of London. However, as scientists, they saw these failures as part of the perfecting process and left the site knowing that their final refinement had been successful. At the factories in Germany, production went to full scale, manufacturing the long awaited super weapon that would bring an inevitable victory to the Fatherland, despite the recent setbacks in Normandy. Dornberger and Braun returned to their laboratories in Peenemunde to continue work on the next stage of the project: the ballistic space rocket.

Over the next three months Londoners were subjected to a new wave of terror. Twenty-four shoppers were killed in Clapham Junction. Thirteen patients, mostly children, were killed when a V1 fell on St Mary Abbotts Hospital in Kensington. One hundred and twenty one of the congregation of the Guards Chapel at Wellington Barracks died when the building suffered a direct hit. Sixty-four American soldiers perished when their transport trucks were hit driving through Chelsea. The British Government played down the casualties to avoid panic, while desperately trying to work out how air defences could be adapted to cope with the new threat. Churchill was eventually forced to admit to the House of Commons that by 15 July 'Doodlebugs' had landed, killing 3,583 people. Not all were on target. One had turned in the opposite direction following take-off and landed close to Hitler's temporary headquarters in Eastern Germany.

Dornberger and Braun were well aware that it was only a matter of time before ways to foil the V1 were found. But they had now completed the design of the first man-propelled object capable of touching the outer reaches of earth's atmosphere. The V2 could obtain a height of 52 miles before it crashed to Earth with a ton of explosives in its nose. Defence was impossible. British command were unaware of this terrifying advance until one of the first prototypes was launched from Peenemunde and landed, not in the Baltic Sea as intended, but in Sweden where it was examined by British aviation experts who confirmed the fears of the intelligence service.

Although the German military hierarchy was aware that a weapon was imminent that could turn the course of the War quickly, and finally, in their favour, disillusion with the Fuhrer had reached a peak not seen since immediately prior to the invasion of Poland. Count Claus von Stauffenberg was not a high ranking officer but his appointment as Chief of Staff to General Friedrich Fromm, who had overall responsibility for the rocket development programme, gave him daily contact with Hitler. Working with a close group of conspirators, Operation Valkyrie was planned whereby von Stauffenberg would smuggle a bomb into Nazi Headquarters. For a military coup to work the appropriate replacement to Hitler would have to ready to take control immediately the Fuhrer was killed. On July 9, Colonel Caesar von Hofacker approached Rommel on behalf of the conspirators at his headquarters at La Roche-Guyon.

Two days later the first attempt to detonate the bomb had to be abandoned when Hitler decided suddenly, as he was prone to do, to move to his east Prussian HQ at Rastenburg. Stauffenberg took the bomb with him. The second planned attempt, on 15 July, was curtailed when Hitler left the room midway through a conference. The next opportunity would be in five days time but things were beginning to unravel. On 17 July Rommel was being driven back from the fighting around Caen when a low flying R.A.F. fighter bomber strafed his convoy with machine gun fire. Rommel survived but was hospitalised with critical head wounds. The conspirators knew they could not turn back and quickly positioned Field Marshal Erwin von Witzleben to take control on Hitler's death.

Stauffenberg was present at the meeting planned for 20 July at which Hitler was due to meet senior Generals to discuss the worsening position on the eastern front. Prior to leaving the room to allow more sensitive information to be discussed, Stauffenberg left his briefcase full of explosive on the table. From a distance of 200 yards he witnessed the explosion that blew up the small wooden hut in which the meeting was held. Stauffenberg immediately left by plane for Berlin where von Witzleben and other senior members of the conspiracy, on hearing the news, had already put their plans into force. They were unaware that seconds before the bomb exploded, one of the Generals present had leaned over the briefcase, in an attempt to get a better view of a map, and taken the full force of the blast. Hitler escaped with nothing more than a minor injury to his right arm.

★

The 109th Battalion of the 28th US Army landed in Normandy on July 22, as part of the second wave of reinforcements, taking the total number of Allied troops in Normandy to a quarter of a million. Two weeks later Caen eventually fell and the push north and west across France could commence. In the meantime another Allied Army of 94,000 men had landed along the Mediterranean coast, between Toulon and Cannes, and was already moving north. The pace of the advance was literally at a crawl, with most of the fighting taking place in deadly steep-sided hedgerows. By 20 August the Keystones had reached Calvados and began a faster and safer progress along the roads towards Paris.

Meanwhile Hitler faced bad news in other areas. On August 9, von Rundstedt's replacement, General Guenther von Kluge had swallowed a cyanide pill. Next to his body was a note to Hitler that read: "If your new weapons, in which such burning faith is placed, do not bring success, then, my Fuhrer, take the decision to end the war. The German people have suffered such unspeakable ills, that the time has come to put an end to these horrors."

A week later, as the Red Army were entering Prussia, the Free French Army arrived in Paris. The first American troops to follow them into the capital were the 28th Army. The famous photograph that appeared across the world's press of American soldiers marching in battle parade in front of the Arc de Triomphe was of members of the Keystone Division who, as a result of their valiant feats in France, had acquired another nickname: The 'Bloody Bucket' Division.

Barely a few days leave was granted to the 28th before they were given orders to continue east through the Forest of Compeigne towards the River Meuse, in the teeth of ferocious German resistance. The Meuse was crossed on September 19, allowing progress into Belgium to increase to an average of seventeen miles a day, although there were still frequent pockets of resistance to be endured. The town of Arlon was secured as the Division fanned out into Luxembourg. Here the battle became still more savage and casualties began to rise again. Eventually the Allied troops, with the 28th still firmly in the front line, crossed the border into Germany.

In battle conditions such as northern France in 1944 many heroes emerge. However, the 109th Infantry Regiment of the 29th Army Division possessed a man whose incredible feats of bravery, both in Luxembourg and Germany, were to earn him his country's highest military honour. Francis Clark was born in Whitehall, New York State into a farming family where he stayed until enlisting. On 12 September 1944, along with his colleagues in Company K, he began fording the Our River near Kalborn, Luxembourg, aiming to take the high ground on the opposite bank. Covered by early morning fog, the 3rd Platoon, in which Technical Sergeant Clark was squad leader, successfully negotiated the crossing; but when the 2nd Platoon reached the shore, withering automatic and small-arms fire ripped into it, eliminating the platoon leader and sergeant, and pinning down the remaining troops now trapped in the open. Clark, from his relatively safe position crawled across a field, through a hail of bullets, to reach the stricken troops. He proceeded to lead his colleagues to safety and then returned into the fire-swept area to rescue a wounded soldier, carrying him while enemy gunfire tried to cut down both men.

Later in the day, having assumed command of both platoons, he led his men in a number of dangerous sorties, weakening German positions with lightening attacks. Clark single-handedly took a machine gun post with a grenade, killing its two occupants. He continued to roam front and flanks, dashing towards hostile positions, killing and wounding an undetermined number of opposing troops, scattering German patrols and eventually forcing the withdrawal of a full, and heavily armed, enemy company.

Five days later, Clark found himself again in the thick of action, this time near the German town of Sevenig. Again, working alone, he attacked an enemy machine gun post, killing one operative and forc-ing the other to flee. When the Germans counter-attacked, Clark's Company suffered heavy losses. Seeing no leadership had survived, Clark again assumed command, constantly moving among his men giving encouragement.

Pinned down in their position the following day, Clark was wounded but refusing to be evacuated, took up a position guarding a pillbox as night fell. He emerged at daybreak, killing the German soldier setting up a machine gun five yards away. Spotting another enemy gun, he moved towards it and killed two Germans with rifle fire. Later that day, despite acute pain, he again braved heavy fire to take food and water to an isolated platoon. When he was eventually repatriated to America Francis Clark was awarded the Congressional Medal of Honour.

On 2 September, two months after he had been sacked, von Rundstedt was once again reinstated by Hitler to take overall command of western forces. The seasoned General knew exactly how desperate the cause was, a conclusion in which Hitler was beginning to join him. Hitler was, however, already planning a military offensive, and remained confident that his weapon of mass destruction would soon be ready.

By the beginning of September British air defences had began to get the better of the Doodlebugs. They were only aircraft and could be shot down by fighter planes and anti-aircraft fire. Weary Londoners had become almost blasé as Doodlebugs sailed over their heads, knowing that the danger only came when the buzzing engine stopped and was replaced by a banshee-like screech as the rocket fell out of the sky.

On 8 September Churchill declared the danger over. He, of course, now knew that a much bigger danger was imminent. Two months before he had chaired a War Cabinet meeting that had warned that as many as 2,000 V2 Rockets, each capable of taking less than four minutes to reach their target, were almost ready to launch. His spies over-estimated the production level, but on the shores of the Baltic, Dornberger and Braun had got the V2 ready ahead of sched-ule. On the same evening the first two rockets landed on London, killing three. News of the new weapon was kept from the press. Churchill's hopes were pinned on his land troops, and old fashioned bombers, being able to cripple supply as soon as possible. If not then the order would be given to use chemical weapons in response. The following week Churchill was at President Roosevelt's home on the River Hudson discussing the progress of America's atomic bomb. The shape of war was soon to change for ever.

In the meantime, the British authorities faced an older and more mundane problem: there were now upwards of 100,000 German prisoners of war in captivity.

10. CAGES

The number of prisoners of war in British hands had built steadily since Major Scotland brought eighteen back from Dunkirk. The first large numbers resulted from the successful British advances in North Africa in 1941. The prisoners were predominantly Italian initially, but as Rommel obtained more and more reinforcements, by the end of the campaign the intake was approximately half German.

Both Major Scotland's PWIS and Major Crockatt's CSDIC had set up regional presences both in North Africa and the Far East. The processing was exactly as envisaged during the abortive European invasion of 1940. PWIS took as much advantage as possible of the first 48 hours of captivity to illicit information before transferring the more interesting prisoners to CSDIC for ongoing interrogation. The bulk of the prisoners were then either transferred back to camps in Britain, or British-run units in Egypt, India or Canada. Low category prisoners tended to be sent to Britain as they could be safely used for labour, though the choice of destination depended much on where the next empty troop-carrying ship was heading.

By 1943 a quarter of the labour working on British roads, farms and construction programmes was provided by POWs. The system worked well. Low ranking soldiers, almost all conscripted, were more than content to work in relative comfort and safety, as opposed to being sent as tank fodder to the dreaded eastern front. The British public, on the whole, recognised that these conscripts were no different to their friends and relatives fighting overseas, or in increasing numbers, being held in German and Japanese POW camps.

From the start of the war the British press had tended to single out Hitler, and to a lesser degree Goering and Goebbels, as being personally responsible for the conflict. Italy was deemed to be single-handedly controlled by Mussolini, who was portrayed as Hitler's puppet. Headlines, from both high- and low-brow papers, almost always used the term 'Nazi', which promoted a distinction from mainstream German people. Generals such as von Rundstedt and Rommel tended to be treated differently to the Nazi hierarchy, the British press giving them almost a grudging degree of respect.

At the start of the war Parliament passed a Non-Fraternisation Law, aimed, in part, to prevent the public having dealings with enemy prisoners of war and internees. By 1945 this law was openly ignored as many low risk prisoners had been working in various communities for up to four years, and as the work tended to be agrarian the rural population had not, in the main, been directly exposed to continued bombing, or had to suffer the loss of their children as evacuees. In contrast dangerous Nazi officers, committed to escape, were isolated in special camps, usually in remote areas.

The success of the Allied invasion meant that the plans, carefully laid by Scotland and Crockatt four years beforehand, at last swung into action. Within weeks of D-Day upwards of 100,000 Germans were in British hands. In North Africa and Italy each Army had tended to handle the prisoners it took, American and Commonwealth regiments all using similar methods to the British in the immediate aftermath of capture. However, prior to D-Day it had been agreed that all POWs from this new theatre would be a British responsibility.

A five-tier system existed to take the prisoner from capture to one of the many new POW camps being opened across Britain. The capturing unit, many of whose Officers would have received basic interrogation training, disarmed prisoners and gathered any documentation in their possession. Wounded prisoners were despatched to designated field hospitals. PWIS Officers then began questioning prisoners as soon as possible in mobile Unit Collection Points that constantly moved a few miles behind the advancing frontline.

Prisoners were then transferred to a Brigade Regulating Point holding 'cages', situated in more permanent locations, usually near to embarkation points along the coast. By now officers and other ranks had been separated. Very often this resulted in lower ranks releasing information, sometimes inadvertently. The POWs were then transported, now under Military Police guard, across the Channel to southern England.

The three Divisional Cages set up at the beginning of the war were soon unable to cope with the volume and a single, massive transit camp for rank and file prisoners was established at Kempton Park Racecourse, on the south-western edge of London. At the Divisional Cages the questioning was more structured. Three areas, tactical, operational and strategic were explored. More was to come in the POW process. Up to this point, any prisoner who had shown himself to be in possession of important information was fast-tracked to the specialist interrogators at CSDIC. The final step, before placing the prisoner in a camp, was to subject them in any event to Crockatt's intelligence division, operating out of three Command Cages: Swindon, Aylesbury and for special 'guests', at Cockfosters and Kensington.

All the thirty or so CSDIC Officers spoke fluent German, often gained as a result of living in Germany on business or in education before the war. To the credit of both Scotland's and Crockatt's departments very few complaints were made that they breached Geneva Convention rules. Many of their officers prided themselves that they often gained important information without their subject being aware that they had provided it. Unlike their British counterparts, German officers had not received any anti-interrogation training. Nazi High Command did not condone surrendering.

Not all information was gleaned by mind games. All of the Command Cages contained microphones hidden in the walls of rooms that were used to put two or three officers together, usually under the guise that they would only be together for a very short period. Two officers, who had been captured in North Africa in 1943, were thrown together briefly in one such room in the Central London Cage. One commented that he was surprised to find that the new weapons he had seen being tested had not flattened London. This was the first inkling British Intelligence had of the V1 rocket.

The dispatch of prisoners to an assigned camp was the final stage. By now they would have been graded as White, Grey or Black. As the colours suggest, White was 'anti-Nazi' and could possibly be persuaded to work with the Allies, usually as an informant within a camp. These were very few in number. 'Blacks' were deemed to be die-hard, fanatical Nazis, almost all the S.S. In between were the largest number, 'Greys': conscripted soldiers, sailors and airmen who, although loyal to Germany, did not demonstrate unfailing allegiance to Hitler. In fact, at this stage of the war, disillusion with the Nazis, and an acceptance that the fight was lost, was the prevailing state of mind in the rump of the German military.

As German prisoners began arriving in Britain the major logistical problem was finding accommodation. Four hundred new camps opened during the second half of 1944. A further hundred would be added before the war ended. Officers and lower ranking German POWs remained broadly separated, although not entirely. Each rank and file camp contained a small number of officers who would retain an element of control and responsibility over the lower ranks. Each officer's camp was provided with a number of ordinary troops to carry out daily tasks for the more senior men, such as cooking. The small numbers of senior German officers in captivity were even allowed to retain a batman. Although Nazi supporters had been identified, the British authorities decided not to segregate camps. Accordingly each camp contained an element of S.S. and non-S.S. officers. A number of German prisoners, not supportive of the Nazi cause, would die in captivity as a result of this decision.

With Allied military resources still stretched well beyond capacity, the War Office also faced the problem of finding a sufficient volume of troops to guard the increasing number of camps. It would be misleading, and unfair, to label the soldiers that served as POW camp guards as not being able-bodied, but the majority of them were of an age, or a category of fitness, that rendered them unsuitable for front line service. A favoured source of guards, especially for the higher security camps, was foreign troops such as Poles. German soldiers who had served in Eastern Europe were under no illusion that these guards would strictly adhere to the Geneva Convention if pushed.

★

When the American troops left Island Farm in April 1944 the site was considered ideal for a low security POW camp, and it became Camp 198. Although the twenty buildings designated for the Germans provided better than average POW accommodation, there had naturally been no need to provide security measures to prevent the original munitions workers, and latterly American troops, leaving of their own free will. Fencing was hastily erected, although the camp's security status was graded as 'low'.

The first inmates were a mixture of low ranking Italian and German prisoners who were immediately assigned to local labour projects, mainly land work in the farms surrounding Bridgend. Soon after the autumn harvest ended, the prisoners at Island Farm were assigned to work that must have amused them. They were tasked with increasing the camp's security by building two large barbed wire fences around the entire two-mile perimeter. When the job was completed the entire detail of prisoners were despatched to other, low-security camps. The First Directorate of the Department for Prisoners of War, the relevant part of the War Office, had taken the decision to convert Island Farm to a top security camp that would house up to 2,000 German Officers.

Superintendent William May, of Mid-Glamorgan C Division, had been the senior police officer in Bridgend since the beginning of the war. A Welshman, born in 1893, he had ambitions of becoming a lawyer when he first entered the police force. His early promotions coincided with the violent pit strikes during the 1920s. Now one of the most respected policemen in south Wales, Bill May had more interest than most in the war coming to an end: his son Harold was being held as a prisoner of war in the Far East.

The Superintendent did not consider the upgrading of Island Farm to be among the best pieces of news he had received during the conflict. At the earliest opportunity May briefed his colleagues at the Bridgend Report and Control Centre situated in Merthyr Mawr Road, less than half a mile away from the camp. The control centre had been set up at the very start of the War and was designed as a central point of contact between the Police, Fire Brigade, Ambulance Service, Army, Home Guard and Air Raid Wardens.

Having the largest munitions factory in Europe in its area, and with other targets such as Cardiff, Swansea, a main railway line to London, and the coalfields nearby, the regular exercises undertaken by the Control Centre possessed a real edge. For four years May had overseen dummy runs that implemented prepared plans for every perceived eventuality. There were detailed, documented plans to counter gas attacks from the sky, German invasion across the sand dunes to the south of Bridgend, and parachuted gangs of saboteurs intent on destroying the arsenal. Gradually the realistic threat of these situations receded, but now May had to design a new plan: one that responded to German Officers escaping from Island Farm.

As word spread that Bridgend was to host a top security POW camp, public fears mounted. These prisoners were not the harmless Italian and German soldiers who were no different to 'our boys', but hardened Nazis. The type whose fanaticism was responsible for the increasing number of atrocities being reported in the newspapers. They may include the pilots who had dropped bombs on south Wales.

Many of the German officers who approached Bridgend in the middle of November 1944, on a specially commissioned railway train, fitted the stereotype that people in Bridgend expected. The non-S.S. officers among them may not have shared an undying loyalty to the Nazi cause, but they still resembled what most of the British public expected a German officer to look like. Discipline and an appearance befitting their status, were ingrained deep into the psyche. Despite the rigours of capture, and the constant movement between what must have seemed like numerous holding camps, the officers travelling to Island Farm had the demeanour of an advancing Army.

Escape plans were already being made. Regardless of the degree of their loyalty to Hitler, the ignominy of capture did not fit well with the average German Officer. Although the treatment they had received at the hands of the British had probably not been as harsh as expected, especially for those that had served on the Russian front, the experience of having their liberty removed would not have sat comfortably with them. Whether the reasons were a sense of duty to the Nazi cause, the expectation of their rank, national pride, or the simply the restoration of personal dignity, the natural reaction was to plan an escape.

Until they saw their prison it was pointless making detailed plans, but most of the men travelling on the west-bound train into Wales would have been making mental notes of the unfolding geography. Luftwaffe prisoners had an advantage as many would have committed to memory maps of Britain. For others, the Great Western Railway Company provided assistance. At the start of the war, when every signpost and public map had been painstakingly removed from sight, someone had forgotten to take down the tourist maps on display in Great Western carriages. One S.S. officer, Karl Ludwig, was quick to spot the assistance that the display above his head would provide to escape plans. As lookouts were hastily positioned to alert him when one of the guards walking up and down the carriage approached, Ludwig was quickly copying the map onto the tail of the shirt he had removed.

As the train pulled into Bridgend Station it was met by a contingent of guards from Island Farm. Superintendent May had sent a number of his police officers to ensure there was no problem from the increasing number of people making their way to the station to get their first look at Bridgend's latest residents.

The sergeant in charge of the guard brigade ordered the disembarking German Officers to assemble so that a head count could be taken. A command structure amongst the Germans had already become apparent and orders were passed around. Satisfied that the numbers tallied with those expected, the sergeant ordered that they pick up their kit bags and begin the march to Island Farm, a distance of about three miles. Not one German Officer moved. The sergeant repeated his order, and was faced with the same response. May's

Policemen watched the stand-off nervously.

A German Officer came forward and explained, courteously, to the sergeant that all the men present were officers and were not accustomed to taking orders from a low-ranking soldier. As the stalemate continued a tall figure in a peaked cap embroidered with gold braid approached. Made aware of the situation he gave a command, in English but delivered in a rich Welsh accent, ordering the Germans to begin marching in the direction indicated by the Guard Patrol. There were no further objections and, to the bemusement of the local policemen, the Germans set off in the direction of Island Farm. Mr. Hill, the Stationmaster, watched as the Germans disappeared down Station Hill and continued to his office where he removed his braided cap.

The German officers proceeded to live up to their image. They marched impeccably, and arrogantly, through the town centre and out along Merthyr Mawr Road towards the camp, loudly singing 'Deutschland Uber Alles'. A small number of schoolchildren catcalled. Some adult residents hurled abuse. May's men feared the worst when a local woman stepped forward and spat in the face of one of the Germans, but the Officer did not react. As the first contingent of German troops marched through the recently-erected, barbed wire-encrusted gates into Island Farm, Bill May knew that his problems were just beginning.

11. PLOTS AND PLANS

Lieutenant-Colonel Edwin Darling was a natural choice to be Commander of the upgraded camp at Island Farm. At fifty-one he was considered too old for combat duty, but he spoke German and his thirty years service included first hand experience of a POW Camp. He had been captured during the First World War and held in a German POW camp from which he escaped and returned to his fighting unit via Holland. A career Army officer, he had spent most of the period between the wars in India and the Middle East where he saw active service in Afghanistan. He was also part of the British forces dispatched to post-revolution Russia and was awarded the Military Cross. His stature, good looks, constantly worn monocle and exemplary manners fitted perfectly the image of an old school, colonial British officer and gentleman.

On arriving at Island Farm he was far from impressed by what he found. Priding himself that he knew the tricks of the POW trade, he was appalled at the glaring security problems that were apparent. Although the hastily erected fences were just about adequate, there was no lighting of any sort around the long perimeter, much of which stretched out into dark, wooded countryside. Darling had expected sentry towers to be placed at regular intervals, equipped with moving searchlights and booster beams that could be quickly directed on anything suspicious spotted by the elevated guards. There was no path laid around the perimeter fence, which meant that patrols would be wading through mud if they were to maintain constant surveillance around the camp. The prevailing soil presented another problem: it was perfect for tunnelling.

Up to this point of the war, top security camps had tended to be situated in remote areas, such as Scotland and the Lake District, for two good reasons. Many escape attempts had fallen at the first hurdle with the fleeing prisoner being unable to survive in the harsh conditions during the initial manhunt. Secondly, as it was widely believed that a primary objective for an escaping German prisoner was sabotage, it made clear sense to situate camps as far away as possible from any sensitive targets.

For a prisoner getting out of Island Farm, the gentle, and quite reasonably populated countryside, presented ample cover in the immediate aftermath to an escape. Not that cover would be needed for that long, with so many road and rail links nearby. Two of the major ports in the country were within two days walk, with smaller harbours such as Porthcawl even closer. An escapee committed to sabotage would be spoilt for choice. Apart from the biggest arsenal in Europe less than two miles away, and still working at maximum production, there were also two massive steelworks and dozens of coalmines within the vicinity. In addition three airfields, the training centre at St Athan and the fighter bases at Llandow and Stormy Down could be reached on foot within a day. Darling promptly made his concerns known to both the War Office in London and his Army superiors at Western Command Headquarters in Chester. His next priority was to meet with Superintendent May.

The primary responsibility for the capture of any escaping prisoners of war was given, throughout the war, to the police force. Up until the opening of Island Farm the police could rely on support from the Home Guard, but May was disturbed to hear from his friend, Colonel William Llewelyn, that the volunteer force was about to be put on a reduced footing. Llewelyn shared May's concerns about the new P.O.W. camp and promised that he would do what he could to ensure that his Bridgend Regiment remained as intact and ready as possible. Both men had made visits to the upgraded camp and were aware of Lieutenant Colonel Darling's initial concerns.

By the end of November 1944, there were already rumours of dastardly sabotage being conducted by escaped prisoners. After a particularly wet autumn, torrential rain prevailed throughout the third week of November. On the weekend, the River Ogmore, which flows through Bridgend at a fast pace even during normal conditions, burst its banks. Within an hour the town centre was under eight feet of water. Bill May realised the looming danger and immediately called in assistance from the Army and Home Guard. Panic had already set in as military vehicles drove through the floodwater to rescue terrified residents waving for help from upstairs windows. Casualties were ferried to hospital and the town centre was evacuated. WVS workers distributed tea and blankets at an emergency centre set up in the Town Hall.

Council surveyors could not understand why the river's flood defences had not coped with conditions that were no worse than had been experienced during other bad winters. One of Bill May's constables returned to the Police Station with the answer. A large tree trunk was wedged across the arches of the ancient hump back bridge in the village of Merthyr Mawr, three miles down stream of the town centre, and within yards of the far end of Island Farm.

By the beginning of December, Camp 198 was full and its latest occupants were acclimatising themselves to their new surroundings, paying particular attention to the opportunities presented for escape. The lower ranking prisoners were billeted in the four huts that ran alongside the A48, Swansea to Cardiff trunk road. The guards' quarters lay between the road and the gate to the main camp. What had astonished Commander Darling, and no doubt gave heart to potential escapees, was that the concrete huts that were to be used as sleeping quarters were mostly situated around the outside of the camp, some within twenty yards of the perimeter fence.

The camp was roughly the shape of an isosceles triangle with its apex pointing south and the base running along the main road. The southernmost hut had been converted into a cookhouse and officers' mess. The middle of the camp was a large open area to be used as a parade ground for the daily roll call. A smaller building next to the eastern edge of the fence had been turned into a church. Another similar sized unit, overlooking the parade ground, was designated as a dentistry and medical centre.

As was normal in both British and German camps, the prisoners were left to sort themselves out. In Camp 198 a command structure, not entirely based on rank, quickly became apparent. S.S. Officers took charge. It was decided that each hut would have an S.S. presence to ensure that Nazi discipline was maintained, and any talk of the war being lost was, literally, stamped out.

Escape plans were already being co-ordinated. The prisoners included a number of officers from Organisation Todt, the state controlled civil engineering organisation responsible for all major construction projects in Nazi-controlled countries. In similar fashion to the scientists involved with rocket development at Peenemunde, the senior engineers at Todt were technically officers in the German Army. Island Farm contained a number who had been responsible for the construction of the U-Boat bases on the Atlantic coast of France. Their practical skills and knowledge could be put to good use.

The senior officers in the camp invited suggestions for methods of escape. Some of the more fanciful suggestions were dismissed at an early stage. These included rigging up a form of chairlift from the electricity pylons on each side of the perimeter fence, a double pole vault by a particularly athletic inmate, and the construction of a hot-air balloon. There was ample opportunity for a handful of prisoners to cut through the fence and make a dash to the nearby woods, taking full advantage of the lack of lighting and inadequate night time guard patrols. Although a handful of POWs might get away, it would inevitably lead to tightened security and was thus discounted.

Another group of prisoners had already reported on the ample availability of materials such as wood and metal implements provided for cooking and gardening. With the experienced Todt engineers on hand, the prevailing type of soil and most importantly, the position-ing of the huts so close to the fence, there was an obvious method of escape. The old chestnut of a tunnel.

A plan began to come together. A tunnel, so well constructed that it could accommodate a mass breakout, would be dug. The Todt engi-neers carried out initial surveys. A properly shored up and ventilated tunnel, from an outlying hut to the other side of the fence could be constructed in three to four months. The soil dug out would need to be redistributed but there was a ready solution available. A patch of land next to the parade ground had been set aside as a small garden area to grow produce for the kitchens. The bulk of the excavated soil could be carefully redistributed there.

As a safety mechanism against discovery becoming a complete catastrophe, and given the ready supply of materials and manpower, it was decided that two tunnels should be dug simultaneously. This threw up an obvious problem: how to dispose of twice the quantity of earth. There were two solutions put forward. The first was to persuade the Camp Commander that the garden area was insufficient and should be at least doubled. The second solution, put forward by a Todt Officer, was altogether more ingenious.

Commander Darling pointed out that if the garden area was increased, there would be less space for an athletic ground-cum-foot-ball pitch, but agreed to the request. He also agreed to the prisoners constructing a long jump pit, not realising that this would be another refuge for redistributing soil.

When the prisoners had first arrived at the camp, many had taken delight in the orchestrated singing of patriotic German songs. Darling assumed that this was a temporary act of defiance and would quickly subside. He was wrong. The singing continued not only during the day when the men were exercising on the athletic ground, or lining up for meals, but also every night, sometimes until dawn. Darling was unaware that the choral activity was taking place at the command of the senior officers to cover the noise of digging.

The prisoners had now to choose which huts to use for the tunnels. The tunnel needed to come out in as dark an area as possible, and one that was close enough for the escaping prisoners to make a short dash to the nearby woods. The two units that were best positioned, needing the shortest length of tunnel, and providing the safest dash to the woods, were Hut 16 and Hut 9.

As Christmas approached, Darling received a response from the War Office to his demands for extra resources. He was reminded that there was a war on. The reply was not totally unexpected and the Commander had already been working on improving security. A rough path had been laid around the perimeter fence with duckboards covering the areas that held excessive rainwater. Intermittent acetylene lighting, mounted on five-foot poles, had been positioned in the darkest areas, but they were insufficient to illuminate more than a few feet of the fields beyond the wire.

By now, Darling had been able to assess the capabilities of the soldiers under his command. He was not impressed. They were none too diligent and tended to do only the bare minimum required of them. What Darling was not fully aware of was that many of his guards were taking full advantage of the abundance of pubs in the nearby town. The prisoners had already gained the upper hand physiologically, by making the guards continually aware that they were inferior in all ways, including rank. The result was that the guards only tended to venture into the main camp area when absolutely necessary.

The Commander's relationship with the senior German officers was civil enough, although they had made Darling aware from day one that they were fully conversant with their rights under the Geneva Convention. They made sure that food rations were maintained and any supplies being brought in from the outside were delivered on time. The only positive news from the first two months of the camp being upgraded was that the spate of escape attempts that Darling was expecting had not materialised. In a way he wished they had, as it would have added weight to the demands made to his superiors. Darling hoped that the apparent reluctance to escape was indicative of a tacit acceptance from the prisoners that, given the state of the war, escape was pointless. The real reason was that the senior officers had given instructions to the men that no individual attempts should be tried in order to protect the mass escape being planned.

Superintendent May's immediate problem was the string of complaints from nearby residents to the constant singing, and jeering of passers-by from the prisoners. Resentment in the town was building, especially when letters in the local paper began appearing that pointed out that the food rations received by the prisoners, which of course was their right, was actually more than currently being made available to the British public.

May had visited the camp on a number of occasions and refined his plan to deal with escaped prisoners. He believed that a mass escape was more than likely and had the utmost respect for the ability of the German officers when it came to the qualities needed to evade capture. Aware of his limited resources, and taking advantage of the public-spirited nature he knew prevailed on his patch, May's plan was based around involving as many members of the public as possible. On 26 December he circulated his thoughts to all police officers under his command:

> The prisoners are highly trained military personnel and would practise military field technique to its fullest extent, and it is to meet and defeat this that the policeman should set himself. This, of course, is something different from the usual police routine but in the efficient policeman the alert mind is also receptive to new ideas. If its alertness is tuned up to the right pitch it will be able to grasp new situations quickly and carefully work out and apply what is to the best advantage in all emergencies.
>
> First of all, it should be recognised that the escaping prisoner has opportunities for sabotage in abundance in this division. Therefore the method of dealing with the hunt and capture of escapees will necessarily have to be considered on its merits in the light of the circumstances as they are likely to arise in each case. The informants constituting information points on the respective beats should be encouraged to repeatedly search and examine their premises and to keep an active observation on all points. When reporting any information every detail should be included; particularly the location of suspects; approximate number; whether the prisoners are on the move or static and whether their attitude as far as it can be observed is merely one of avoiding capture or of violently resisting recapture.
>
> A constant search patrol should be maintained, linking up with the various military points, furnishing the military personnel with all possible information collected in the course of the patrol and from the information points.

Immediately following a report of an escape, all pedestrians and motorists not known to the police should be called upon to produce their identity cards and upon being proved correct they should be warned of the escape and their co-operation sought by reporting the movements of any suspicious persons or incident on their journeys to the police.

Whilst there is now no legal obligation there is a moral obligation on the part of the public, particularly on the occasion of a mass escape of prisoners of war, to immobilize cars, cycles, lorries and any other vehicle. Failure to act promptly in this respect will give the escaped prisoners the chance to provide themselves with transport from unattended vehicles or vehicles in insecure garages. It would be all to the good if the readily removable parts could be taken away from the vehicle for the time being.

The prisoner's greatest advantage against his pursuers will be his highly developed military instinct to adopt all forms of subterfuge. To beat him, one must have a perfect knowledge of the countryside and be able to find one's way about just as well by night and in fog as in broad daylight. To attain this the pursuers should have the qualities of: a good hunter; be able to improvise and make quick decisions; never to tire when following up information received; suspect everything; be on the alert; once the alarm of an escape is given, to reconnoitre unceasingly.

Bill May was at pains to point out to his men that while they were to encourage people to assist by making their vehicles immobile at night, they were not to make the rising panic any worse. The war was nearly over, and the Germans would soon be going home. However, on the Western Front, the German Army was making a final, desperate roll of the dice to turn the war back in their direction.

12. A Last Roll of the Dice

There was very little warning as a V2 Rocket plummeted from the stratosphere. In regular bombing raids the dull drone of the approaching wave of planes and the staccato cracks of anti-aircraft fire were heard a long while before the pounding thud of distant explosions came closer. The lunchtime shoppers in Deptford, south London, queuing patiently with ration books on a cold November lunchtime, would only have had a couple of seconds warning before the rocket struck. Moments later 160 people lay dead.

The V2 had, however, not brought the level of destruction anticipated by both Churchill and Hitler. With superiority of the air, and consistently supplied with good intelligence, the R.A.F. Bomber Command had managed to destroy a number of the rocket factories and launch sites. The German response was to hastily open new factories, and find new sites to launch from, although options were becoming increasingly limited as Allied troops swept across northern France and into Belgium and Holland. The effect was that the volume of rockets falling across England neither increased nor abated until the spring of 1945. The capital continued to take the brunt: 585 Londoners were to be killed in January, another 483 in February.

On 15 December 1944 Field Marshal Montgomery wrote a letter to General Eisenhower, his Commander in Chief, enclosing an account for a bet struck the previous year. Eisenhower wrote back saying that there was still another nine days for the war to end and the wager to become due. Six months before, both men would have settled for the progress made since D-Day. The Allied front line now ran from The Hague to the Swiss border. It was a time for the Allied troops to regroup and snatch what little enjoyment they could from a Christmas spent in a war zone. For Allied Command, the festivities were to be used to plan the next, and hopefully final, offensive of the War. The only realistic line of German defence between the front line and Berlin was the Rhine. The carnage on the Eastern Front continued, but the Red Army was making steady progress across eastern Germany. The obvious wager for the New Year was which Allied Army would reach the German capital first.

As Montgomery and Eisenhower were settling their bet, Hitler was addressing a meeting of his Youth Leaders at his 'Eagle's Nest' bunker in Bad Nauheim, close to the Western Front. "Never since the Napoleonic wars," the Fuhrer told them, "has an enemy devastated our country, and we will decimate this enemy also at the very gates to the Fatherland." Acknowledging the closeness of the Allied frontline, Hitler went on to assure his faithful following that it was on this front that Germany was "going to turn the tide and split the American-British alliance once and for all."

This was not hollow rhetoric from a desperate Fuhrer. He had personally planned a massive and audacious counter-offensive. A superstitious man, there was more than a degree of *déjà vu* about his plans. He had last used Bad Nauheim as his HQ during the glorious *blitzkrieg* of May 1940. The location of the counter-offensive was again to be the Ardennes Forest, and the man to be given overall command was the General Hitler had relied on more than any other throughout the War: Gerd von Rundstedt.

The veteran General, now approaching the age of 70, had set aside the humiliation of being blamed for the failure to repel the Allied landings in June, and once again dutifully answered Hitler's call. Von Rundstedt was one of the few Generals whom Hitler did not suspect of being involved in the attempted coup of the previous summer. Not so Rommel, who, while he was recovering from his wounds, received a visit from two S.S officers. They carried a personal message from Hitler, who offered Rommel the choice of immediately taking a cyanide pill or facing a public trial. Rommel chose suicide.

On 4 December, a PWIS interrogator had elicited from a recently captured prisoner that a major German offensive was being planned. Nevertheless, Allied Higher Command totally underestimated the scale and immediacy of the danger for a number of reasons. The German Army had been in retreat for so long that the Allies could not conceive that anything more than increased resistance was a possibility. When an Army has been on the offensive for so long, the mistake of assuming the enemy can never take the initiative is a common one. If the Germans were planning an offensive it would almost certainly take place against the Allied troops moving towards the industrial Ruhr. Finally, with von Rundstedt back in command, strategy would be orthodox and cautious.

Although von Rundstedt had been given the title of Commander-in-Chief for the West, in fact he had very little direct involvement in the Ardennes offensive. Hitler had entrusted his plan to a younger, much less conventional officer: General Hasso von Manteuffel. At 47, von Manteuffel was young to have reached such a senior rank. Starting the war as a Lieutenant, he quickly earned a reputation as an exceptional tank commander during the German offensive in Russia. From there he was transferred to serve under Rommel in Tunisia, before returning to the Eastern Front where he had been wounded in August 1943.

Hitler's plan, codenamed Operation Greif, the German for the mythical griffin, was a reworking of the Trojan Horse stratagem of Greek legend. Von Manteuffel was to be given a small, crack, troop of English-speaking commandos who, dressed in American uniforms were to cause havoc behind Allied lines, prior to an advance by two panzer armies. Hitler chaired the final conference of his commanders at Bad Nauheim on December 12. By now von Rundstedt had fully digested the Fuhrer's plan and considered it unworkable. In its favour were an element of surprise and that it appeared to be attacking the Allies at their weakest point. It was estimated that there were only 80,000 U.S. troops in the area against a quarter of a million Germans. In addition, weather reports indicated that low cloud and fog, typical for the Ardennes in mid-winter, would prevail for at least a week, meaning that the Allies would enjoy only a limited benefit from their superior air cover. The flaw in the plan was the depth to which German resources had been depleted over the last six months. Von Rundstedt concluded that the reason the plan would fail was that by the time Allied reinforcements arrived, German fuel and ammunition would have run out. Hitler was gambling on his Army breaking through any resistance within the first few days and pushing the front onward to Brussels and the port of Antwerp.

Von Rundstedt, from first hand experience, knew that it was pointless to attempt to change Hitler's mind. All of the senior military men were horrified that Hitler had presented them with a finalised plan so detailed that they were even told the exact method and timing of the attack. Von Manteuffel, having the least experience of Hitler's intransigence, naïvely, but successfully, argued for a number of practical changes to be made. He pointed out that commencing artillery fire three and a half hours before the infantry attacked would only "wake the Americans up". He also had devised a plan that would allow for the initial wave of tanks to be able to launch their attack before the customary time of early light. The conference closed with the attack being set for 16 December.

Although winter was closing in, there had been little respite for the

28th Infantry Division after they crossed the German border during the first week of November 1944. They were given the task of clearing the Hurtgen Forest. The 'Keystoners' stormed into the towns of Vossenack, Kommerscheidt and Schmidt, encountering stiff resistance at every point. Losses and casualties were heavy as ground was often taken, lost and retaken. However, ten days later they had successfully completed their mission.

Fresh orders promptly arrived and the 28th moved south. Here, at least, they were not faced with mounting another offensive. They arrived in the Ardennes forest where they were to defend a strategically vital stretch of the Allied frontline, along the Our River. Christmas was approaching and the men, who had been in active combat now for five months, could at least look forward to a period of regrouping before the next forward push.

In the early hours of December 16, thirty-three German commandos, fluent in English and wearing US flak jackets, drove stolen American jeeps into enemy territory. Through the night they roamed around unchallenged, cutting telephone lines, swapping around signs and taking away the red warning tapes signifying German minefields. Their penultimate task, completed at around 5.30 a.m., was to set up a line of powerful searchlights that shone directly up to the sky. Taking advantage of the low cloud cover, each light reflected down over a wide area. As fuel depots exploded, the first wave of German tanks crashed through the frontline, now brilliantly lit up by von Manteuffel's 'artificial moonlight'.

The American troops were immediately in disarray. Frantic messages were dispatched to Eisenhower's headquarters in the Versailles Palace, on the outskirts of Paris. Allied Command hung on to their belief that a full scale German assault in the Ardennes was impossible. It would take them a crucial 24 hours to comprehend what was happening, and another two days to properly respond.

Realising what had caused the initial chaos, American troops set up roadblocks to prevent any further German sabotage. By nightfall on the second day of the offensive, German tanks had progressed further than he could have hoped for. By now von Manteuffel had assumed – wrongly as it transpired – that Allied reinforcements would be heading towards the Ardennes. His hopes rested on his tanks bursting through the hopelessly outnumbered American defences and heading towards the coast by the time that the Allied reinforcements arrived.

As dawn broke on the second day of what became known as the

'Battle of the Bulge', pockets of American troops throughout the Ardennes had dug in to their defensive positions, knowing that their task was to hold back the German advance for as long as it took for reinforcements to arrive. As news spread of an event that had occurred the previous day, a firmer spirit began to take hold. The cry 'avenge Malmedy' was shouted from soldier to soldier.

Malmedy is a small Belgium town, in the northern reaches of the Ardennes, about twenty miles from the German border. The first German troops to arrive there on the morning of 17 December were an S.S. unit led by Lieutenant Colonel Joachim Peiper. After a fierce fight, seventy-two Americans were captured, marched into a field and shot. Peiper's unit carried out another ten similar massacres on its western advance, killing at least 308 Americans and 111 Belgian civilians. The following year, when he was brought to account at a post-war trial, Peiper claimed that Hitler had given orders to every unit involved in the Ardennes offensive that the thrust should be preceded "by a wave of terror". His defence was not supported by the fact that there were no such allegations made against any other German units involved in the battle.

Four days later, at Chenogne, near to the market town of Bastogne, where US troops were under siege, twenty-one German troops emerged from a burning house, waving a Red Cross flag. They were gunned down by American troops. General Patton, one of the American commanders in the conflict, wrote in his diary on 4 January 1945 that there were "some unfortunate incidents in the shooting of prisoners (I hope we can conceal this)".

Although the dank weather continued to prohibit any relief from the sky, the American resistance gradually began to slow von Manteuffel's progress. It had taken Allied Command three full days before they accepted that they were being faced with a major German offensive. 180,000 troops were urgently added to the 60,000 originally dispatched to the area, an even smaller number than the German estimate. This delay should have been more than sufficient to allow von Manteuffel to reach the coast, but the American resistance had ensured that by 23 December even his most westerly tanks were still short of the River Meuse. As dawn broke that morning, von Manteuffel was faced, for the first time during the offensive, with his worst nightmare: a clear blue sky. The pockets of besieged American soldiers scattered throughout the Ardennes were given the Christmas present they were hoping for. Wave after wave of Allied planes began striking at German supply lines and fuel depots. Prior to the attack, von Manteuffel had been adamant that, based on his experience in Russia, the figures produced by the tacticians at German High Command had completely underestimated the fuel requirements for the offensive. Even before the clearing weather, the German tanks were already beginning to run short of fuel. Within hours, up to 5,000 bombers were demolishing German supply lines.

Within days the German advance had ground to an enforced halt. Von Rundstedt would not have been surprised at Hitler's response to his request that an immediate retreat to the Eifel Mountains be conducted. Four divisions of the British Army led by Field Marshall Montgomery had now joined the American forces and the Allies began pushing the German frontline backwards. By now the unauthorised German retreat was in disarray with tanks being left where their fuel ran out and the crews retreating on foot

The final German counter-offensive of the war in Europe was over. Allied troops began regaining the lost ground, and by the middle of January were again ready to begin the push across the Rhine and then on towards Berlin. Hitler left for the capital but broke with his customary sacking of von Rundstedt following a humiliating defeat. The General was given the task of regrouping the German forces to mount a defence of the Rhine. As in Russia three years beforehand, von Rundstedt was left to count the cost of the needless losses that could have been avoided with an orderly retreat.

Yet Hitler's gamble had nearly paid off. Had American resistance been anything short of heroic, von Manteuffel may well have reached his goal before his fuel ran out, the weather cleared and the Allied reinforcements arrived. The 109th Infantry Regiment, and the whole of the 28th Division had held their position against the odds. Their defence against the five crack German divisions thrown at them during the first day of the Battle of the Bulge, followed by another four divisions attacking over the next few days, earned one war correspondent to describe it as "one of the greatest feats in the history of the American Army". Their immediate reward was to be dispatched to another front line.

13. Conflicting Messages

Information is the most vital commodity to a prisoner of war, though it is said that the first casualty of war is the truth. The two decades leading up to World War Two had seen the birth of modern media and the Nazi government used every new facet available to make sure the German people, and the military, consistently received the desired message. Up until the turning point of the War it was not necessary for Hitler's propaganda machine to control news of events on the war fronts, only to conceal the increasing number of atrocities occurring behind the lines. From 1942 onwards all news needed to be manipulated. Details of the carnage on the eastern front were kept to a bare minimum. The Allied invasion of Italy was presented as the capitulation of a weak ally. Rumours of concentration camps were dismissed as British propaganda. By the middle of 1944, the message was that the Third Reich would still emerge victorious from the Allied onslaught.

The majority of prisoners at Island Farm had been captured in France and Belgium during the five months following D-Day. To them, there could be no doubt that a very large Army had successfully landed in France and made steady progress towards the German border. Individual assessments of the war differed greatly. To the majority of S.S. officers, defeat remained inconceivable. Large numbers of non-S.S. troops were still confident that the mighty German military machine would eventually triumph. Others had drawn the conclusion that an Allied victory was now inevitable. Views of Hitler ranged from dogmatic and unfailing worship, to the growing realisation that he was desperate, if not mad.

As the prisoners settled in to their new surroundings at Island Farm they were all anxious for news, both of their families and the progress of the War. Unbelievably the Red Cross continued to maintain its remarkably efficient postal service that ensured prisoners on both sides gratefully received a steady trickle of mail. The British government did not have the resources to censor incoming letters, beyond an occasional random check, and accordingly the news messages received by the German public were being passed on to prisoners in Allied hands.

There was another form of more direct communication. The

POWs at Island Farm included a number of technicians and, very quickly, a handful of homemade radios were lashed together. With the German government still in control of some of the most powerful radio transmitters in Europe, these basic receivers were capable of picking up the constant messages deliberately broadcast in their direction. The crackling programmes continued to give up-beat news. Both Allied fronts had now ground to a halt. The still superior, mighty, German Army had regrouped and was taking delivery of the mass of new weapons that were being churned out of the production lines, unaffected by sporadic bombing. In addition, London was being systematically destroyed by wave after wave of V2 rockets, a weapon far more advanced than anything in the Allies' arsenal.

The British press had been allowed a degree of freedom throughout the war, the government relying on the combined patriotism of the B.B.C. and national newspaper owners. Laws had been passed that prohibited newspapers printing sensitive information such as troop movements and even weather forecasts. In the first phase of the war the press dutifully informed the public of the constant stream of bad news with typical British understatement. Politicians opposed to the war struggled to find outlets for their views. As the tide turned, a degree of triumphalism began to appear.

By November 1944 there were nearly one million German POWs held in Britain. The Government felt that if these men were made to feel defeated they would be easier to control. The Political Welfare Unit was formed, a specialist department that was to co-ordinate a propaganda campaign initially, and then carry out a structured 'de-Nazification' programme.

As Christmas approached, the prisoners at Camp 198, Bridgend, were struggling to make sense of the conflicting messages to which they were exposed. As soon as the Ardennes offensive started the German media reported events as a magnificent success for von Rundstedt's Army. Within days there were reports of the Allies suffering heavy casualties and retreating in confusion. This metamorphosed into their fleeing towards the coast with von Rundstedt in pursuit, their only hope being a second Dunkirk. In the meantime, London was ablaze for the umpteenth night and any of the Russian Red Army that had not already starved to death were now surrendering.

Prioritising officers, the Political Welfare Unit printed thousands of newsletters, written in German, and distributed them throughout the POW camps. Hastily erected public address systems loudly broadcast the British version of the news, read in German, to the prisoners. At Island Farm some prisoners would have read, and all would have heard, of a desperate German rearguard action in Belgium that been quickly reversed. Hundreds of German tanks had been abandoned and the all-conquering Allied Army was continuing its advance toward the weakly-defended Rhine and then on to Berlin. There they would meet with the vanquishing Russian Army that had already liberated Poland. In addition, R.A.F. Bomber Command, with the skies now practically to itself, was sustaining the constant bombardment of Germany's industrial heartland.

As in most camps, the S.S. officers held at Island Farm took responsibility for both discrediting the British propaganda and ensuring, one way or another, that morale was maintained. Orders were given prohibiting the mention of anything other than an inevitable German victory. These paradoxical messages led to prisoners being driven to escape by a number of motives. The diehards wanted to return and continue the inexorable drive to victory. Others wanted to answer the Fatherland's call in the hour of greatest need. Many, especially those from the bombed out major cities in northern Germany, or the east of the country now occupied by the dreaded Russians, were desperately concerned about the fate of their families. Those who felt the war was over feared for their treatment at the hands of the Allies. There were rumours that all German prisoners were to be handed over to the Russians and dispatched to concentration camps. Many wondered how British treatment would change when there were none of their prisoners in German hands. Little wonder that escape was so important to a German prisoner at the end of 1944, and at Island Farm plans were well underway for the mass breakout.

Another feature of life in a POW camp is that groups of strangers, many traumatised by recent events, are thrown together under stressful circumstances. The German Army, the Kriegsmarine, the Luftwaffe and the Waffen S.S. were all products of their own culture. Now men from these different parts of the military were forced to live together in cramped, basic conditions. This pressure cooker has the capacity to produce anything from violent friction to the forging of lifelong friendships.

Commander Darling had been instructed that there were to be no S.S.-only huts in Island Farm. Hut 9, the unit chosen for one of the two tunnels, contained a mix that was typical throughout the camp. The ranks went from the lowest officer rank to Commander. One in

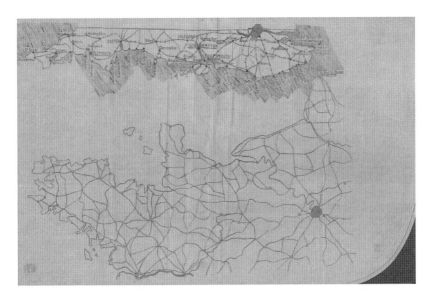

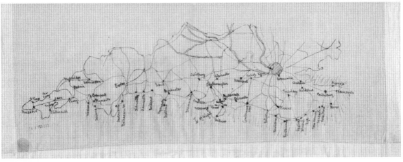

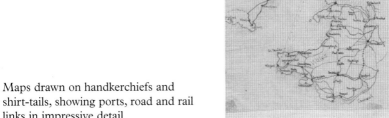

Maps drawn on handkerchiefs and
shirt-tails, showing ports, road and rail
links in impressive detail.

Left: 'Porridge Man' – artistic mockery of prison guards.
Above: the tunnel exit; escapees returning under guard.
Facing page: Police and troops scouring the countryside, as photographed for the *Western Mail*.

Superintendent William May, senior police officer in Bridgend and Lieutenant-Colonel Edwin Darling, Camp Commander.

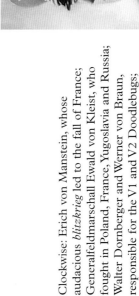

Clockwise: Erich von Manstein, whose audacious *blitzkrieg* led to the fall of France; Generalfeldmarschall Ewald von Kleist, who fought in Poland, France, Yugoslavia and Russia; Walter Dornberger and Werner von Braun, responsible for the V1 and V2 Doodlebugs; Walther von Brauchitsch, one-time Commander in Chief of the German Army.

Generalfeldmarschall Gerd von Rundstedt at Bridgend Railway Station and (below) with his son and Lieutenant-General Alexander M. Patch.

Top: officers line up to salute von Rundstedt as he leaves for Nuremburg.
Centre and bottom: SS and Kriegsmarine Officers at the Camp.

German Officers helping with the harvest; (top right) with a group of orphans; (below) the Island Farm Camp.

five of the men were S.S. The most senior officer in Hut 9 was Oswald Prior, a U-Boat Commander who had been captured in Le Havre, on the west coast of France, a month after D-Day. If anybody had been equipped for living in close confinement with others, it was a submariner. Since arriving at Island Farm, Prior quickly became friendly with two fellow hut-mates. Hans Harzheim, an anti-tank commander, exuded a calm, almost laid back manner. Fluent in English, since his capture he had taken to reading any British newspaper he could lay his hands on. Werner Zielasko was a tough man, not S.S., but typical of the patriotic rump of the German Army which continued to support Hitler and believed that the Third Reich would still emerge victorious. The three men all had their own reasons to escape and immediately volunteered to work on the tunnel.

The team organising the escape had decided that although it was to be a mass breakout, the prisoners would make their getaway thereafter in groups of three and four. Each group would have a leader and preferably include an English speaker and a pilot or seaman.

One of the last prisoners to arrive at Island Farm, just before Christmas, was Oberleutnant Steffi Ehlert, a twenty-four year old Luftwaffe officer. Pilots were a top priority to include in any escape. Not only because they were desperately needed for the German war effort, but they also provided the means for the quickest route back: stealing a plane. As a reconnaissance pilot, Ehlert, who held a map of Britain and France in his head, carried an even higher premium. Commander Prior wasted no time recruiting him into his group.

Karl Ludwig fitted the image of an S.S. officer. Tall, well built and blond, a product of the Hitler Youth, he had proudly joined the German Army in 1936 as an eighteen-year-old. Already a hero in the camp for quick wittedly copying the map he spotted on the train, Ludwig made it clear that he and Heinz Herzler, a fellow S.S. officer, would make their escape without anybody else in their team.

The planning stage of the escape was completed by Christmas. The Todt engineers had calculated that each tunnel would take four months to complete. While the tunnels were being constructed, the time would be used to store up sufficient food rations to sustain each escapee for at least three days. Senior German officers had informed Commander Darling that they would take over the task of distributing food rations to their men. The escape rations were creamed off before the daily allowances were handed out to the camp. A team of men was assigned to accumulate civilian clothing. It had already been decided that each escapee would wear his German uniform underneath a coat that would pass at least a cursory glance. This way, unless the British were prepared to break the Geneva Convention, anybody caught could not be shot as a spy. Another team was to produce identity papers that, again, would pass a crude inspection. The remaining task was to make copies of Ludwig's map. With a collection of basic tools assembled, the digging of two tunnels could now commence.

As he celebrated New Year Eve at the local Conservative Club, Commander Darling and other revellers must have thought that 1945 would finally see the end of the War. Darling would also be glad to see the end of his latest command. He had by now concluded it was going to be a tough one.

Darling had become increasingly despairing of the guards under his command. With one or two exceptions, they were undoubtedly the shoddiest group of soldiers he had encountered during his long military career. The reasons they were guarding POWs varied, but none were there as a result of their military prowess. Darling intuitively knew by now that escape plans were being hatched, but the only attempt he had discovered so far was a hole in the fence that some of his guards were using to nip out for a quick pint of beer during their watch.

The guards had also lost, hands down, the psychological war with the prisoners. The German officers, particularly the S.S., naturally maintained an air of arrogant superiority. They had created a climate that made most of the guards feel inferior. Some were downright intimidated. Many ensured actual contact with the prisoners was kept to a bare minimum. On most days it was no more than the 9.00 a.m. roll call. Even this event was controlled by the prisoners. The Germans would choose between marching to their posts with military precision, always singing patriotic songs, and a leisurely line up at their own pace, surlily ignoring the guards' orders. Both tactics were orchestrated, manipulative and designed to show to the guards that it was the POWs that maintained the upper hand.

Very often the roll call would result in the headcount being short and the alarm being sounded. A frantic manhunt would ensue, and always result in the missing prisoner(s) being found either asleep in a bunk, sitting on the toilet, or carrying out some mundane task, seemingly oblivious to the need to stand and be counted. Darling recognised the tactic, a classic one, which he recalled from his Great War experiences. It was designed not only to waste the guards' time, but also to take them eventually to a point of complacency that would pay dividends when a real escape took place. Darling's problem was that the only punishment that could be meted out to the prisoner, whose turn it was to play hide and seek, was one or two days in solitary confinement.

The prisoners also derived immense pleasure at night from throwing stones out of their huts at the fence, causing panic amongst the hapless guards. Again deliberately designed to drain the guard's resolve, this ploy resulted in the first death at Island Camp. A guard, on hearing a crack against the barbed wire, shouted for the figure disappearing into the darkened field to halt. In line with his training, after making a mandatory attempt to call for the escaping prisoner to stand still, he opened fire. The terrified sheep, running from the noise, was killed instantly. When hearing the guard's version of the incident it highlighted another problem to Darling. The makeshift lighting may have illuminated the few feet each side of the fence, but being at head height it was impossible for a guard to see beyond the glare into the fields beyond.

Although the prisoners had settled in, the camp had not settled down. The singing was almost constant into the early hours. The prisoners had also taken to a structured ritual of loudly banging their tin plates and knives and forks together every time they assembled for meals in the canteen. Another contributor to the racket was the noisy plumbing system, tested to the full by a co-ordinated, and continuous flushing of each toilet in sequence.

The senior officers also enjoyed the upper hand over their camp Commander. Darling was faced with regular visits where streams of demands were made, always strictly in line with the Geneva Convention. His patience was tested to the limit when it was pointed out that the rules entitled all officers to sheets. When Darling became aware of an escape plan that had been foiled in another camp, he hoped that Western Command would now address his concerns. He would be disappointed.

Camp 23, in Devizes, Wiltshire, had been upgraded around the same time as Island Farm. During the last week of November 1944, two separate pieces of information were collected by British Intelligence. Piecing them together foiled a daring escape attempt in Devizes, but also very nearly ensured the German offensive in the Ardennes succeeded.

MI19 had an informer in Camp 23. Within weeks of the camp being opened, he passed on sketchy details to his contact that a large escape was being planned. More importantly the intention of the escapees was to capture a nearby Army base and use the arms there to return to the camp and free all 7,000 prisoners. Having caught his handler's attention, the informant followed up with more detail a few days later.

The breakout was planned for Christmas Eve and it was now apparent that the prisoners in Camp 23 had detailed knowledge of the local area. The Army camp being targeted was in possession of a number of Sherman tanks that were used for training exercises on nearby Salisbury Plain. The prisoners also knew of an American fuel depot, an airfield and a central food store. After Camp 23 had been liberated, other POW camps in the area were to be attacked. This was not an escape, but a full-blown military offensive, starting in the heart of southern England.

Major Crockatt now had a team of men working on the information, which was coming through in piecemeal fashion. Knowing the escape was not to take place for another month, and desperate to identify any assistance being provided by German agents outside the camp, Crockatt had agreed with Southern Command that no action be taken at this stage. The informant then passed on a final, extraordinary, fact. The escape was going to coincide with a team of paratroopers being dropped into the area on the night of the escape.

This information fitted perfectly with, and appeared to corroborate, a coded message intercepted at Bletchley Park on 30 November. Hitler had personally ordered the formation of a unit of paratroopers for special duties on the Western Front. Each man must be fully trained in hand to hand combat, speak fluent English, be familiar with American dialect and have a good knowledge of military technical terms. The newly formed unit would be commanded by S.S. Obersturmbannfuhrer Otto Skorzeny.

Alarm bells now rang at full volume. It was tempting to allow the German plan to go ahead and capture the infamous Skorzeny at the same time, but the danger of the plan actually succeeding, or being brought forward without sufficient warning, outweighed the temptation. A company of the 8th British Parachute Battalion, on training exercise in Britain, stormed into Camp 23 on the afternoon of 14 December. The ringleaders were rounded up and taken to the London Cage for further interrogation. A week later British Intelligence realised why Skorzeny's crack troops had been assembled.

Although it did not result in extra support for Commander

Darling at Island Farm, the enormity of the plan at Devizes, even without paratrooper assistance, prompted the War Office to accelerate a programme to nullify Nazi resistance in the camps. The many interrogations conducted by PWIS and MI19 had given the British a deeper insight into the mentality of those with diehard loyalty to Hitler and his regime. They looked on Hitler's plans as the formation of a German empire that would last for a thousand years. Many had grown up knowing nothing other than a country controlled by the Nazi Party. Those who remembered the social and economic problems before Hitler came to power still thanked the Fuhrer for bringing order and prosperity to Germany. Very few prisoners were aware of the atrocities that were being carried out by the S.S.

Lieutenant Colonel Henry Faulk was appointed to design and implement a de-Nazification programme to which all German POWs would be subjected. Faulk's starting point was that German prisoners needed to be taught the difference between Nazism and patriotism; that it was possible to be a loyal German without subscribing to the extremes of Hitler and the Nazi Party.

Faulk's team, many of them with a teaching background, visited the camps giving enforced lectures. The German media had, for years, portrayed British democracy and parliamentary systems as being corrupt and ineffective. Prisoners were shown how it worked; the more responsive were invited to take part in mock parliamentary debates. Those that showed no interest were forced to view pictures and cinefilm of concentration camp victims and Russian prisoners, that had emerged from Eastern Europe. S.S. hardliners maintained that the pictures were either produced in Hollywood studios or filmed in famine stricken India.

The long term objective of Faulk's work was to re-educate prisoners in advance of post-war repatriation. In the short term it was hoped that it would address increasing violence in the camps as S.S. men struggled to maintain the party line. A number of deaths had occurred, particularly in officer camps. Darling was not the only commander that pulled a wry smile as he was ordered to stretch his limited resources to prevent any further occurrences of Nazi discipline and intimidation taking place. Whatever measures Commander Darling took, they did not save the life of one officer at Island Farm.

14. ONWARD AND UPWARD

Inspector May was in the process of refining Plan X when he heard about the escape plot at Devizes. He was more concerned to hear from Commander Darling that the events in Wiltshire had not led to extra resources in Bridgend. Darling made it clear to May that he was under no illusion that the camp was escape proof. May had long held the same opinion. Worse news followed for the policeman when he was informed that without any threat of a German invasion, or the prospect of renewed bombing raids on south Wales, the Bridgend Control Centre was to close on 8 January 1945. May knew this would make the response to an escape more difficult as his plan was based on being able to mobilise as many people as possible to throw a three-mile cordon around Island Farm. It now became even more essential that if an escape could not be prevented, it was at least discovered as quickly as possible.

The tunnelling work in both huts was now well underway. The basic tunnel designs were almost identical. A vertical shaft of eighteen feet would end in a space large enough for two men to stand and pass each other. From there, in the case of Hut 9, the tunnel would gradually progress upwards to the surface. The angle of ascent was calculated so that the sixty-foot passage would exit in the small copse on the other side of the fence.

Without attracting attention from the guards, oak benches were taken from the canteen to the hut, where they were sawn up and used to support the sides and roof of the tunnel. The shaft in Hut 9 descended from the area at the southern end of the building, originally designed as a living space. The guards were told the room had been adapted into a dormitory for senior officers, as it possessed heating. Apart from providing an excuse to conceal the shaft entrance with a bed, this also meant the room was less likely to be inspected. When tunnelling work ended for the day, concrete dust was carefully sprinkled over the slab of stone covering the entrance.

As well as providing the tunnellers with meticulous plans, the Todt engineers had devised an ingenious method of disposing of the bulk of the excavated soil. Halfway along the hut was a large shower and toilet area. A completely false wall was constructed using scavenged bricks, which were laid and bound together with porridge. The makeshift mortar was brought into the hut each morning by a cook carrying a large pot, which the guards assumed was being used to serve the senior men breakfast in their quarters. With the wall completed, the clay extracted from the tunnel was rolled into small balls and dropped into the cavity between the real and fake walls.

The excitement of the escape attempt, along with the phenomenal amount of work required, had produced a spirit of camaraderie in Hut 9. Other group leaders had come forward, and already onward plans from Bridgend were being made. Helmhart Perl, a naval midshipman from Dusseldorf, decided to head to one of the major ports nearby, either Cardiff or Swansea. Hermann Schallenburg, like Steffi Ehlert, a Luftwaffe pilot, was trying to work out on his map where various airfields might be located. With so many men making for the Welsh ports, Oberleutnant zur See Sund Rolls was going to head for the south coast of England. Given the distance, he was given permission to travel with one companion.

Gerhard Fiegal, at nineteen the youngest man in Hut 9, had survived the Russian front only to be taken prisoner in Le Havre soon after D-Day. A studious, bespectacled young man, he had no over-whelming desire to escape, but felt obliged to join his fellow officers. The slightly built Army Officer, Carl-Heinz Brockmeyer, was the comedian of the hut, but his chirpy manner belied the worry he carried for his family in Hamburg, knowing of the regular pasting that the German port was taking from Allied Bomber Command.

With Commander Prior's group, all the men enthusiastically took their turn at the tunnelling. The younger, fitter men took on the bulk of the work, with the older officers organising an elaborate warning system beginning on the far side of the camp. In the unlikely event of a guard venturing into the compound, let alone having the audacity to enter a hut, the shaft could be closed and covered within minutes.

As the tunnel progressed the length of time that each prisoner could spend underground in a space that was practically pitch dark and lacking in air became an increasing problem. The Todt men had been working on a solution, which they completed just as the breathing difficulties were bringing work to a standstill. Each hut was supplied with a ventilation system constructed out of empty tin cans, stuck together, that connected the workface with a fan made out of four blades wedged into a bucket. The device was hand operated from the hut. It allowed a tunneller's shift to be extended from two minutes to fifteen, although Steffi Ehlert was amongst the victims who had to scramble to the surface when the fan operative's digestive problems forced an emergency evacuation.

Inspector May's problems were not confined to preventing escaping Germans getting out of Wales. On top of the incessant din emanating from Island Farm, word had got around the town about the amount of provisions being driven into the camp on a daily basis, along with details of how the prisoners enjoyed their own bakery, the use of a gym, a library and a theatre. For the local residents these stories coincided with news of the conditions British prisoners had been forced to endure in German POW camps recently liberated by the Russians. In addition, the first, sketchy information about concentration camps was beginning to emerge. All this while London, and several other English cities, continued to suffer significant casualties as a result of rocket attacks. Bill May began to fear, not for the Glamorgan public if there was an escape, but for the escapees themselves.

Some of the prisoners were indeed enjoying the use of a gymnasium but the background to its establishment highlighted an increasing problem in the camp. One of the smaller buildings had been designated as a church and, as with other camps, the authorities had ensured that Island Farm contained a German military padre. A group of S.S. Officers decided that the church was to be converted to a gym, exclusively for their use. The padre complained to Darling. This resulted in the S.S. informing the clergyman that it would be in his interests to withdraw the complaint and request an immediate transfer to another camp for his own safety. The replacement Padre was content to conduct his services in the canteen.

S.S. bullying was now rife in most officer POW camps. There had been a number of deaths but investigations by the British authorities always met with a wall of silence. Questions were now frequently asked in the House of Commons regarding how a relatively small number of S.S. men were able to impose their will on other prisoners.

Commander Darling had a limited number of options to deal with the issue. Many of his guards were afraid to even count the prisoners, let alone discipline them. Other camps solved the problem by allowing Polish guards a free reign to ensure order. Without this resource, Island Farm was a camp, like many others, that took the view that the problems were a matter for the Germans to sort out themselves.

Soon into the New Year of 1945 an S.S. initiative began spreading around many POW camps. Each prisoner was to sign a birthday card, add an individual message, and post it to their Fuhrer. Some cards even included a donation of Reichsmarks. Apart from a massive display of loyalty, as the exercise was within a prisoner's rights, it would also place an enormous strain on the British postal system.

Two examples, taken from other camps, demonstrate the extent of the loyalty the S.S. were demanding and getting, even at this stage of the war:

> My Fuhrer
> On your 56th birthday I wish to send in my name, and in the name of all comrades of Camp 21 and Compound D, our best birthday regards. We hope that our Lord may give you, our Fuhrer, strength and health to lead our Army to a glorious victory and a just peace. May you continue to lead our beloved native land to peaceful recovery. Although with hands bound, our hearts believe in you, my Fuhrer!
> Heil Hitler!

> On the occasion of the 56th birthday of our Fuhrer, we send you with our birthday regards a donation of RM 327,230 in the name of all the German soldiers of Camp 21 as a sign of our unbroken loyalty to our Fuhrer and our nation, as a birthday present for our beloved Fuhrer.
> We think about our brave German homeland, and we are sure that we shall gain a heroic victory in spite of very grave misfortune.
> Long Live the Fuhrer; Long Live Greater Germany
> Heil Hitler!

The increasing calls for loyalty to the Nazi cause were too much for one, middle aged, officer at Camp 198.

Otto Iskat had endured prisoner of war camps much harsher than Island Farm. Born in Vienna in 1895, he had served in the Austro-Hungarian Army during the First World War. After being awarded three bravery medals, Iskat was captured on the Eastern Front and was imprisoned in a camp in Siberia. As the Great War merged into the Russian Revolution, he was released but not repatriated. Iskat spent two years travelling through a war-ravaged Europe to get home. Being fluent in thirteen languages helped him complete the journey.

After gaining a degree at Vienna University he worked in the construction industry until the Anschluss unifying Austria and Germany. Finding himself now working for Organisation Todt, Iskat, in line with other senior engineers, was made an officer in the German Army. He was assigned to the building of the gigantic U-Boat facilities in the French Atlantic coastal port of Brest. Using forced labour, Iskat supervised the construction and ongoing operation of a complex of buildings large enough to house thirty submarines at any one time. A twenty-foot thick concrete roof, capable of withstanding the direct hit of a 2,000-ton bomb, provided protection. By the time of the Allied invasion of northern Europe, Iskat had climbed to the rank of Oberregierungsbaurat (Lieutenant Colonel). He was still at his post when the Americans arrived. After a month-long siege, the German forces at Brest surrendered. Iskat was taken into captivity brandishing papers that confirmed he was a civilian construction official. The Americans did not accept their validity and two months later he found himself at Camp 198, Bridgend.

A deeply intelligent, intellectual and artistic man, he busied himself in captivity by painting and writing poetry. Art was prolific through-out the camp with prisoners using the concrete walls of their huts as canvases for watercolours and oils. Many of the images were to remind the men of their own particular homeland. Scenes of Bavarian forests or Alpine landscapes adorned the camp. Another source of inspiration, or perhaps desperation, produced portraits of scantily-clad women, reminiscent of the type Americans painted on their bombers. The light hearted and picturesque impressions were balanced by numerous swastikas adorned with the eagle emblem of the Third Reich.

By this stage of the War, a great many of the prisoners at Island Farm were disillusioned with Nazism, though very few of them chose to make this known to any but their closest colleagues. However, Otto Iskat did nothing to contain his disenchantment, much to the chagrin of his fellow officers still loyal to the Nazi cause. On the morning of 26 January 1945, he was found dead in his bunk. His body was taken to Bridgend Hospital where the cause of death was recorded as Acute Syncope, a form of recurrent and sudden fainting. It will never been known if his death was directly or indirectly caused by Nazi hard-liners striving to maintain discipline within the camp.

With the assistance of crude air-conditioning, work on the tunnels had continued throughout January. An exceptionally cold month ensured guards were a scarcity. Engineering advances included sleds on pullies, which speeded up the removal of soil from the workface, and electric lighting wired from the huts. The proliferation of artwork in the camp was used to good effect in Hut 9. For any guard minded to make a perfunctory inspection, his attention to the shaft entrance under a bed was diverted with a particularly graphic female image on the wall above. By this stage he would also have missed the ironic humour of a caricature of 'Porridge Man,' carrying his daily bowl of nutritious adhesive to the false wall.

The backroom operation, squirreling rations, altering clothing, copying maps and forging documents was on schedule. A greatcoat belonging to the Great Western Railway had somehow been acquired. The large brass buttons, decorated with an official-looking logo, were used to stamp forged identity papers. One of the prisoners had come up with an ingenious design for compasses. Used razor blades were magnetized, balanced on a pin and mounted on small blocks of wood. By the end of January, with both tunnels past halfway, estimates were for the escape to take place in early March. Then disaster struck.

Two British soldiers attached to a frontline regiment found themselves temporarily stationed at Island Farm. They were immediately given the hated job of inspecting the huts. Differing from their new colleagues insofar as they were keen to impress their superiors, they went about their task with a degree of thoroughness that the prisoners were not used to. By the time the two guards arrived at Hut 16 the early warning system had worked to a degree and the shaft was covered by its usual concrete hearthstone. It was the hurried sprinkling of concrete dust that attracted the attention of the two new brooms. The alarm was raised and Commander Darling was sent for. When he arrived, Darling himself climbed down the shaft to be confronted by a naked German close to suffocation.

A full-scale inspection of the camp took up the rest of the day. To the amazement of the prisoners in Hut 9 their tunnel was not discovered, but any delight was marred by the confiscation of the bulk of the escape rations and equipment. Commander Darling was still not content. He knew that tunnels were invariably dug in pairs and although Hut 16's twin had not been found, immediate measures were needed to tighten security.

Darling implemented a second daily inspection to take place at midnight. This served two purposes. Apart from aiding security, it also served as an ongoing punishment to both the prisoners and the disgraced guards who had allowed the tunnel to be built under their noses. Within days a fence had divided the main compound with a large gate in the middle. Although the gate was left open throughout the day it was used to shepherd the prisoners through every morning to ensure a more accurate headcount.

In Hut 9, the prisoners took stock of events. It was agreed that the completion of the tunnel should be progressed at an even greater pace. The danger of it being discovered by one of the new style inspections far outweighed the fact that many escapees would now have to make their onward journey with minimal practical assistance. Another factor was that however recent news from the war was interpreted, and whatever each individual's personal reasons for escape were, the incentives were becoming overwhelming.

*

While most of the Allied land troops on the European western front were regrouping in advance of a spring offensive, the 28th Infantry Division were seconded to the First French Army. Their orders were to capture the last remaining major French town under German occupation. Colmar, fifty miles south of Strasbourg, and less than ten miles west of the Rhine, was strategically crucial for both sides. After eventually driving back the Ardennes offensive, a pocket of German resistance around Colmar represented the only obstruction to the Allies' preparation to cross Germany's mighty western river border. Not surprisingly General von Rundstedt had ensured the troops defending the town were the best available. Hitler's unequivocal orders to them not to surrender would have come as no surprise.

On 26 January the 109th Infantry Regiment led the Franco-American assault on the town. Fierce fighting raged for the next thirteen days. By the end of the battle 1,600 French, and 540 American, soldiers lay dead. 22,000 German troops were taken prisoner, and the Allies now controlled the entire west bank of the Rhine. For their endeavours, the 109th were awarded the coveted French Croix de Guerre and ordered to rejoin the American Army and prepare for the next offensive.

The stage was set for the final phase of the war in Europe. Hitler's ambitions were now confined to a German empire that faced the Allied Army across the Rhine and the Red Army across the River Oder in the east. To the south, the Alps protected the Reich from the Allied troops occupying most of Italy. Hitler remained defiant. His astrologers told him that destiny would dictate a victory. His scientists at Peenemunde were telling him that they would soon have a jet propelled bomber not only capable of reaching New York, but also carrying Hitler's long awaited atomic bomb.

Despite the successes since D-Day, Allied Command was under no illusions about the difficulties that lay beyond the front line and on the road to Berlin. The weather dictated that the offensive must wait at least another month, so the decision was taken to utilise their control of the air and totally destroy what remained of Germany's industrial infrastructure. Four new cities were now within Allied bombing range.

On the night of 13 February, 245 British bombers approached Dresden and dropped their payload. Three and a half hours later, another 529 planes did likewise. With the city ablaze, a further hail of bombs fell the following morning from 450 American aircraft. By now eleven square miles of the city were on fire. The flames burned for seven days. British and American prisoners of war from nearby camps were used to pull what remained of the bodies from the rubble and bury them in mass graves. To this day the total death toll is unknown but generally believed to be in excess of 60,000. The inscription where most of the dead are buried asks: "How many died? Who knows the number?"

15. Get Set

Not even the German wartime press could hide the bombing at Dresden. The British press reported the stark details in its usual deadpan manner. To a prisoner held at Island Farm, whether the news further compelled him to rejoin Germany's fighting forces in its hour of greatest need, or stirred a deeper desperation to return to his family, the need to escape became overwhelming.

Immediately after Dresden, the Republic of Ireland, which had stubbornly held on to neutrality throughout the war, declared its borders open to Germans seeking asylum. For those prisoners at Island Farm who, for whatever reason, accepted that the surrender of Germany was only a matter of time, a major concern was what would eventually happen to POWs in Allied hands. The scaremongers had no doubts. Once Allied prisoners were liberated, German POWs would either be shot by the British, or handed to the Russians for torture before being shot. A more rational train of thought was that repatriation would happen, but when? Very few thought that the day after Hitler capitulated they would be on a plane back to Germany.

Ireland looked an increasingly attractive option, especially as it was relatively accessible from Wales. The escape teams in Hut 9 now fell into two distinct groups. There were those that wanted to return as quickly as possible to Germany, whether it was to fight or to protect their families. Apart from a handful, who had targeted local airfields, these groups would head east into England. Those aiming for Ireland would make for the Welsh seaports of Cardiff, Barry, Porthcawl, or Swansea. There they intended to see out the rest of the war in freedom, better positioned to make their eventual journey home to a defeated Germany.

Commander Prior and his team of Zielasko, Harzheim and Ehlert were determined their return to Germany would be direct. Ehlert, drawing on his reconnaissance experience, had suggested they head to Castle Bromwich, an airfield near Birmingham. His rationale was that as soon as the alarm was raised the various airforce bases in south Wales would be heavily guarded. Most of the groups in Hut 9, including Luftwaffe pilots, were going to take advantage of the direct road and rail links towards London, targeting the numerous airfields scattered around the south east of England. Ehlert and his friends were happy to head north east, especially as the route to Birmingham was across country.

Hans Harzheim had also done his homework. Despite the discovery of Hut 16's tunnel, general security had quickly reverted to its former laxity. Harzheim had managed to slip in to a working party of rank and file men from the other compound. For several mornings he would swap places with a private and use the daily excursion to nearby farmland to build up a picture of the immediate locality. He was more than pleased to share this information with the other escape teams in the hut, but it was on the strict proviso that the Austin Ten car parked each night outside a house in Merthyr Mawr Road, less than 500 yards from the tunnel exit, was theirs. Harzheim had spotted a doctor's badge on the windscreen and knew that it meant that the car would be well serviced and probably full of petrol.

Helmhart Perl and his group were happy to head for the nearest port and then somehow jump, or steal, a boat to take them to Ireland. Hermann Schallenberg was one of the pilots who did not share Ehlert's concerns and was hopeful that security at the local airfields would be porous, especially if he could get there before the alarm was raised. Gerhard Fiegal just planned to get out and take things as they came. The wise-cracking Carl-Heinz Brockmeyer had decided to try for Ireland. After the Dresden bombing, he was even more desperate for news from his family in Hamburg. His jokes belied the fact that he was also increasingly worried about what the Allies had in store for POWS after the War. The naval lieutenant Sund Rols still intended making for the English south coast, and from there onward to the continent and eventually Germany. For the two S.S. Officers, Karl Ludwig and Heinz Herzler, seeing the war out in Ireland did not enter their heads. They would follow a direct line back to the fatherland.

Work on the tunnel had soon recommenced after the Hut 16 catastrophe. The supply of wood began to run low, but sawing exactly the same amount off each bed leg in Hut 9 quickly solved the problem. The shaft and passage had been carefully lined with rags to avoid the escapees emerging with tell-tale clay stains on their clothes during the breakout. As the beginning of March arrived, the engineers calculated that there was less than six feet to the surface.

The embargo on other escape attempts had been lifted after the discovery of the first tunnel. It was now argued that a few escape attempts would not tighten security any further, and might give the impression that there was no second tunnel. In any event there were many disappointed residents of Hut 16 that could not be accommodated into Hut 9's escape and who felt the need to try other means. When two prisoners were caught near to the camp they were manhandled back into the compound. German senior officers complained to Darling about the treatment the escapees received and the guards responsible were given fourteen weeks detention.

Two others got further away. Iron bars wrenched from a hut window were sharpened into a set of crude wire-cutters. After forcing their way through a particularly badly lit part of the fence, the prisoners made their way into the woods. Realising the alarm had not been raised, they then headed west. By morning they had travelled fifteen miles. After resting, they made their way into Port Talbot, a town with a confusing name, as the sea is a mile away. Here two policemen apprehended them.

On hearing the news from his colleagues in the neighbouring Division, Inspector May wasted no time in making his concerns clear to Commander Darling. He demanded to know why the alarm had not been raised for nearly twenty-four hours. The honest answer was that the prisoners at the morning roll call had somehow managed to cover up the escape, despite the new measures introduced. The oversight was compounded by none of the guards immediately noticing a gaping hole in the fence. May reinforced the point to Darling that all the well-laid police plans, designed to capture escaping prisoners, relied on the alarm being raised by the camp without any delay. Darling offered some reassurance. He had at last been given some extra resources.

As the prisoners in Hut 9 were working the night shift, buoyed by the news that the escape was now less than a week away, they heard the noise they had been dreading since work on the tunnel started. They heard a dog bark outside the hut.

*

Any hopes Hitler may have had that space age technology would save him were dashed on February 17 when Allied troops closed in on the research facilities at Peenemunde. Dr Dornberger and his fellow scientists hurriedly collected whatever equipment and notes they could and left on a private train, heading for Bavaria, where Hitler had established a bolt hole for favoured party members. It was the end of the road for their long range jet-propelled bomber.

British Intelligence had also identified the site of Hitler's atomic research facility at the Auer factory just north of Berlin. Now within easy bombing range, the target was given top priority. It would take a month before it was totally destroyed. America's analogous project, codenamed Manhattan, was on course to produce a workable bomb by the summer.

The day after Peenemunde was overrun by the Allies, Hitler awarded General von Rundstedt the Swords of the Knights Cross for his services to the Reich. The veteran soldier had long abandoned any hope of Germany winning the war. His immediate priority was to hold the Rhine defences for as long as possible, without needless loss of life. He felt that when the Allied push came it would be towards the Ruhr. With the Russians now occupying Upper Silesia in the east, if the Ruhr was lost then Germany would no longer have access to coal, nor the ability to manufacture any further weapons. Von Rundstedt gave orders to destroy every bridge across the Rhine.

On the eastern front, the Red Army had already managed to cross the southern end of the Oder River. Starving German soldiers, with no illusions as to their fate at the hands of the Russians, were surrendering in their tens of thousands. Further to the east, in Krakow, the German retreat was little cause for celebration to the 2,000 Poles who were among the first to be loaded onto a crowded train and transported to a Russian concentration camp.

As the month of March brought the first respite to the winter weather, the Allies planned their final advance into central Germany. On 3 March, Winston Churchill flew to the town of Julich to personally view the Western Front. It was the first time a British Prime Minister had set foot on German soil since Neville Chamberlain climbed onto an aeroplane at Munich in September 1938, armed with a sheet of paper ensuring the people of Europe peace in their time. As Churchill addressed the troops, twenty-one V1 rockets, the first since the previous September, struck London.

Two days later, Hitler lowered the age of conscription in Germany to include fifteen year olds. His believed that salvation may yet come from his Youth Movement, who were being told: "It is your duty to watch when others are tired; to stand fast when others weaken. Your greatest honour, however, is your unshakable faithfulness to Adolf Hitler." The country was virtually out of fuel but the Fuhrer remained confident that the Hungarian oilfields could be recaptured. More and more he was relying on astrological predictions that there would still be one defining moment that would turn the War finally towards a victory for the Third Reich.

The 'Keystoners' had not seen any action for nearly a week. After leaving Colmar and rejoining the main American Army, they were tasked with advancing east across the L'Ill River and Rhine-Rhône Canal. Resistance was mercifully light and on the last day of February they arrived at their intended position on the Olef River. On March 6 the orders arrived to push forward to the River Ahr. The 28th Division proceeded to take the towns of Schleiden, Gomund, Kall, Sotenich, Sistig and Blankonheim in rapid succession, capturing large numbers of prisoners and enemy supplies. They regrouped at Blankonheim and awaited their instructions to cross the Rhine.

They were spared having to be among the spearhead troops that crossed the river. Allied Commanders had planned the attack for March 24, basing their tactics on the assumption that von Rundstedt's troops would have, by then, demolished every bridge. However, on 7 March, a small unit of the American First Army raced through a gap in the Eifel Mountains and arrived at the small riverside town of Remagen. The inhabitants hung white flags out of their windows to avoid any conflict, but it was the intact Ludendorff railway bridge that caught the American's attention. On the far side, German engineers were frantically laying explosives. A column of U.S. troops opened fire while running across the bridge. The German detonator failed and the first Allied troops had succeeded in crossed the Rhine. General Eisenhower contacted the unit to congratulate them, denying their Commander's request to proceed to Berlin. When the news reached the London newspapers the following day it was marred by a V2 rocket landing on Smithfield market, killing 110 people.

As American troops were reaching the German side of the Rhine, a tunneller from Hut 9 pushed his small shovel upwards and was faced with daylight. Night time digging had been stopped to prevent an electric light shining out of the tunnel when the breakthrough was made. The Todt engineers had made precise calculations and the tunnel had come out exactly as planned in the small, tree-covered hollow, ten feet the right side of the fence. That night, a meticulously orchestrated operation passed a message across the camp to the tunnel face that the nearest canine-accompanied guard was far enough away from the exit. The small hole to the surface was quickly made big enough to allow one of the prisoners to climb out into the field. He was passed a large stone and carefully positioned it over the hole. Satisfied that it fully covered the opening, without being likely to fall through, he slid the stone to one side and returned down the tunnel. From inside, the stone was gently pulled back over the exit.

A few more days' work was needed to shore up the last few feet of the tunnel and cover the newly exposed clay. Final preparations for the escape could now be made. The weather that week had been fine and mild for the time of year, although temperatures had dipped just below freezing on a couple of nights. Amateur forecasters in the camp, now acclimatised to the idiosyncrasies of Welsh weather, felt that it would remain dry for at least another few days.

Rations for the escape remained a problem. A few groups could be given enough for a week, leaving the others with nothing. Democracy prevailed and it was decided that each group would have at least a few days provision. A plan was put forward that, although risky, might provide a last minute top-up of supplies. Another plan had been devised to nullify the dogs. The night of March 10 was set for the breakout. It was a Saturday and that meant the guards arranged themselves in a way that ensured as many as possible could take their turn to attend the weekly dance in Bridgend. On the day before the escape, while the prisoners in Hut 9 were trying to contain their excitement, dramatic events were taking place on a number of fronts.

That Friday, Hitler telephoned General von Rundstedt and sacked him for the third and final time. The Fuhrer personally blamed the General for allowing the Americans to cross the bridge at Remagen. Hitler declared "I don't want to hear any more about him". He was "finished". Goebbels recorded in his diary that the veteran General "works too much on First World War ideas to master a situation such as is developing in the West".

On the same day as von Rundstedt was receiving his dismissal, U.S. troops were entering Bonn. Although preparations were now at an advanced stage for a bulk crossing, a political row had erupted between British and US commanders. The American breakthrough at Remagen had not fitted in with General Montgomery's well-laid plans. His American opposite number, General Patton was now sweeping north, along the German bank of the Rhine. Since crossing the river there were already another 25,000 POWs in Allied hands.

The Americans were not expecting an attack that morning 500 miles to the west. The Germans had still, against the odds, retained occupation of the Channel Islands, which they invaded in June 1940. From here, on 10 March, they launched an audacious raid on the

French coastal town of Granville. Several port installations were blown up and sixty-seven German POWs were released. The subsequent U.S. military report said that the enemy had succeeded in obtaining "complete control" of the area before they returned to the Channel Islands with a handful of American prisoners.

Thousands of miles to the east, 334 American bombers were heading for the Japanese capital, Tokyo. During a three-hour raid they dropped 2,000 tons of incendiary devices. The resulting firestorm was bigger than Dresden. An estimated 130,000 people died. It was the start of a systematic carpet-bombing campaign by the Americans that would practically destroy the cities of Nagoya, Osaka, Kobe, Yokohama and Kawasaki. To put the American air supremacy in perspective; 243 Airmen would loose their lives during this twelve-week operation, the same number of British lives lost, eighteen months previously, in a single air raid on Berlin.

None of the German prisoners, making final plans in Hut 9 on that pleasant March day, had any idea of the events taking place around the globe in pursuit of winning the war that had put them in Island Farm. In any event, their concerns were firmly focused on a handful of guards, their dogs, and what lay beyond the woods they had been staring at for months.

As Hitler boarded a train that night to make what would transpire to be his final journey to Berlin, sleep was in short supply in Hut 9. The excitement of hoping this would be the last night in captivity was mixed with the host of 'what ifs' that enter restless minds. What if the dogs smell the first head to emerge from the tunnel? What if a snap morning inspection discovers the product of three months hard labour? What if we are caught? What if the British troops decide to take revenge for the fifty Allied prisoners that were shot in cold blood after a similar escape attempt at Stalag Luft III. What if the British propaganda is wrong and Germany could still win the war?

One thing that was certain: tomorrow was going to be a long day.

16. Go

Every year, sometime in March, there comes a day that makes people feel that spring has finally arrived. The presentiment is not just based on the weather; it is a combined sense of well-being that encourages people to collectively look forward. If winter can be likened to a long dark tunnel, then this day is when heads finally poke into the light. In 1945, the feeling was that the tunnel had been particularly dark and long, making the shaft of light particularly bright.

The prospect of the war finally coming to an end had moved from hope to probability over the nine months since the previous June. Very few people dared assume it was over, but on the other hand, the days of Dunkirk and the Blitz seemed a very long time ago. Most of all, it had been five gruelling years since there was such a feeling of normality in the air.

In south Wales, the morning paper of March 10th brought news that the bridgehead over the Rhine now measured ten miles. Allied troops were pouring over the river supported by uncontested air cover and facing little German resistance. The paper's front page went on to give details of the relentless Russian progress to the east, and even further afield, news that Mandalay was on the verge of falling to British and Indian forces. Statistically, German defeat was becoming more and more evident. Hitler had lost a million men since D-Day, including fifty-three Generals.

The positive news from various frontlines set up the day perfectly in south Wales for two eagerly awaited events that reflected the growing return to normal life. Cardiff Rugby Club was hosting a team of New Zealand Servicemen at the Arms Park and, fifty miles down the road at the Vetch Field, Swansea was playing archrivals Cardiff City at football.

For Garfield Davies, however, there were two concerns on his mind as he steadily drove his tractor systematically up and down the field adjacent to the eastern perimeter fence of the prisoner of war camp. First, there had been a worrying report of an outbreak of foot and mouth disease at a farm in nearby Llantwit Major, the second within twenty-four hours. His other worry was the prospect of next week's annual ploughing contest due to take place at Pencoed. Losing to another ploughman was always bad enough, but this year there was the growing consternation that he might lose to one of the Land Army girls. With nearly four years experience, these women could no longer be laughed off as a sideshow.

If Garfield needed a dress rehearsal for his skills in front of a live audience, this morning he was being accommodated. Perhaps these Germans had never seen a field being ploughed before. Perhaps they were impressed with the consummate skill of a Welsh farmer. Perhaps they just had nothing better to do, and after four months were bored witless. Whatever the reason, there were certainly a lot of them staring at his trailing furrows as they moved steadily towards the camp fence.

For the spectators from Hut 9, the focus was on the large stone covering the tunnel exit. Concern was mounting that, after three months hard labour, their plans were going to be brought to a halt by this Welshman and his tractor. Those that knew anything about the art of ploughing were reassuring their more urban colleagues that there was more than enough flat, open, field available to the local farmer to ensure that he did not need to risk driving his tractor into a hollow, and around a copse, just to create two extra furrows. Nevertheless, there was a sense of relief on the prisoner's side of the fence when Garfield decided to call his day's work to a halt ten yards short of the stone.

Most of the German officers counting down time to the early hours of the next day, had experienced, some many times, the excruciating period immediately before going into battle. This, in many ways, felt the same. The difference was that the sense of danger was replaced with a sense of hope, which in turn led directly to the spectre of crushing disappointment if something were to go wrong, either during the escape, or worse, much worse, before it could go ahead.

Not that this mission was entirely risk-free. Hans Harzheim would have noticed the story in the *Western Mail* giving details of a recently attempted escape from a POW camp in Staffordshire. Two Germans had been shot dead, another wounded. They were attempting to steal two fighter planes. The same method of getting back to Germany that Harzheim was planning with Prior, Zielasko and Ehlert.

Other escape groups were also spending the final day going through the detail of their escape. Many of the groups of four had now decided to break away in pairs. It was felt that with rations lower than expected, and the weather boding fairer than anticipated, speed was the priority, especially for those making for England. For the groups aiming towards Ireland, a popular plan was to head for the mountains a few miles to the north of the coast and lay low, maybe even surviving for several weeks in the wild, before jumping a ship when the initial panic had died down. One prisoner had come forward who knew the terrain north of Port Talbot quite well as he had spent an extended cycling holiday there before the war.

Although the sun had not been able to break through the hazy cloud, by mid-afternoon the temperature managed to reach an unseasonal 53 degrees. At the Arms Park, Cardiff were on their way to beating a team packed with All Black internationals by 22 points to 11. Their footballing neighbours from Ninian Park did not fare so well in Swansea. They lost to a last-minute goal.

Trying to appear to the guards as if the day was totally normal, the prisoners busied themselves checking and rechecking their homemade compasses, or staring at their version of Ludwig's map for the umpteenth time. The non-English speakers were being tested one last time on the handful of phrases they had been learning over the last few weeks. As the dim-out time of 7.38 in the evening approached, the two teams who were planning to top up the food rations, and nullify the guard dogs, were getting ready. In the British quarters, Commander Darling was putting on his dinner jacket and preparing to leave for a function at the local Conservative Club.

Soon after Christmas, Herbert Baumann, an officer with an artistic background, had opened the camp theatre. Every few weeks a different production was rehearsed and put on, over a few nights, for the rest of the camp. The show on the night of Saturday 10 March was deliberately designed to be especially raucous, with a guaranteed full house. Baumann was pleased as a series of musical numbers called for full audience participation.

As the entertainment noisily entered its climatic phase, a small group of prisoners broke into the guard's food store. After pillaging as much tinned food as they could carry, the half-empty boxes were carefully resealed and restacked. Back in Hut 9 the extra rations were quickly distributed among the escape parties. For the previous few days a cottage industry had been churning out small pieces of toast, covered in spices, intended to be edible for at least a week.

There had been no curry served in the camp canteen since the guard dogs had arrived. As the storeroom was burgled, another small group of men were also taking advantage of the din coming from the theatre. They slowly walked around the perimeter fence sprinkling pocketfuls of curry powder onto the duckboards that the guards used for their patrols. To test their work, as the audience were leaving the theatre, a few men went to the far end of the camp and stood by the fence. An approaching guard told them to return to their hut and await the midnight roll call. The smiles on their faces as they walked away were due to the evident failure of his dog to catch their scent.

With Commander Darling safely socialising on the other side of town, the guards quickly went through the motions of the nocturnal head count. Pleasantly surprised that the Germans were unusually compliant, and satisfied that everybody appeared to be present and correct, the prisoners were ordered back to their huts for the night.

Faces could now be blackened with soot and ash. Brockmeyer joked that this would have the added benefit of making them all look like Welsh miners returning home from the pit. Messages for friends and families from prisoners not making the escape were being distributed. Lieutenant Rols was briefing the sergeant he had chosen to accompany him. Prior's group were packing their rucksacks and putting on their civilian cloths, trying not to laugh at Zielasko's choice of riding jodhpurs. Ehlert had somehow acquired a much more sensible matching tweed cap and jacket.

Immediately after lights out a small group of prisoners were sent down the shaft to prepare the tunnel for the mass exodus. Word eventually came back that the exit hole was now ready. It was 3 a.m. and the largest ever escape of German POWs was underway.

In the tunnel, the electric light was doubling up as a security system. A network of lookouts was in place across the entire camp. Whenever a guard approached the turn that brought Hut 9 into view, the light in the tunnel was switched off, prompting the conveyor belt of escaping prisoners to make an immediate halt. When the light came back on, the flow of men crawling out of the hole into the copse could recommence. With military precision every time a group of men exited the tunnel, the other groups would move up a place, and a new team drop down the shaft.

The S.S. men, Ludwig and Herzler, were numbers nine and ten to break out. By now the temperature had fallen sharply and was just below freezing. Not that this was really felt by those unfortunate enough to have endured a Russian winter. Ludwig and Herzler quickly took their bearings and sprinted to the woods. Their onward plan was relatively straightforward. After months of observation they knew that the A48 trunk road that ran along the front of the camp was usually busy right through the night with slow moving lorries. Providing they could jump on board a vehicle unnoticed they would be well on their way by the time that the alarm was raised.

Most of the men making east were hoping to board one of the many freight trains they knew travelled throughout the night towards Cardiff and beyond. Plans were simple. Get as far away as possible and then use their wits to decide on the next move. Reaching Cardiff gave a limited number of options, all of which would close down quickly when the alarm was eventually sounded at Island Farm. Everybody hoped their train would continue through the long tunnel that most had encountered when they were originally brought into Wales. Ludwig's map showed that the tunnel ran under the River Severn. If they got this far, they would be in England, near to the large port of Bristol. Further south lay Southampton and Portsmouth. If the train kept moving east then within a couple of hours they would be in London.

Sund Rols and his colleague were also towards the front of the queue. Having made the dash to the woods, they had looked at their next step countless times from the window of Hut 9. They headed due north, across the main road and towards the main London railway line. The men taking this route had agreed to gradually fan out: the later you left, the more your route took you northwest.

With the first dozen prisoners safely away, and excitement mounting, the inside of the hut continued to be a model of efficiency. As each of the groups approached their turn to drop down the shaft they stepped onto a small wooden stool, and were subjected to a double check designed to ensure everyone had their maps, compasses, papers and rations. Nobody knew when the whistle on the escape would be blown. Getting twenty fully-equipped men away would be a remarkable achievement. Every man over that was a bonus, although by then the escapees would be making their way, with minimal rations. Capturing them would, however, take up British resources, meaning the escapees getting away early would stand a better chance. As a military strategy the escape had a secondary objective: to create as much disruption as possible for the enemy.

The men making the last minute checks wished Prior and his three friends good luck. They dropped into the shaft and crawled along the tunnel, realising now the importance of the painstaking amount of work that had gone into covering every inch with rags in order to keep their clothing clean. Like every other man, each of them half expected their heads to be greeted with the barrel of a rifle when they emerged into the field. There was no time for congratulations when they reached the woods, and with Harzheim leading the way they set off to pick up the transport he had promised them.

He led them across the pitch-black main road and into a street lined with houses belonging to the more wealthy and affluent of Bridgend's residents. Harzheim was true to his word, halfway along the street there was a black Austin 10. Pulling a screwdriver out of his pocket, the tank commander set to work on the starter motor. Here the group met their first problem. The car would not start.

Back at Island Farm the groups led by Helmhart Perl, and Carl-Heinz Brockmeyer had also got away and were making the first few steps of their westerly journey towards Ireland. In the hut, the men who had started the escape with fifty of their more privileged colleagues in front of them were beginning to think that they might just get away. After that, who knows?

Prior's group were not the only ones to have problems. Moving slowly along the A48, Ludwig and Herzler had become increasingly frustrated at the absence of any trucks. The two men thought better of flagging down one of the occasional cars that passed and attempting to cadge a lift. The locals were wary that anybody with a vaguely foreign accent was a German POW. Had they tried it with the black Austin that passed with four occupants, they would have been amongst friends.

Harzheim had given up trying to start the Doctor's car with his screwdriver. He suggested his three colleagues push start the vehicle. Merthyr Mawr Road is flat but the weight of the men was just about getting it up to a speed at which Harzheim could confidently slam it into gear, when Prior, Zielasko and Ehlert froze at the sight of three British soldiers walking towards them. The gait of drunken soldiers is consistent within all warring armies. As the soldiers approached, they spotted what was obviously a group of working men struggling to get to whatever job they did for the war effort. Feeling the car suddenly surge forward with double the weight now pushing it, Harzheim took his foot off the clutch and the engine spluttered into action as his bemused friends jumped in. Speeding down Merthyr Mawr Road the bewildered Germans looked back at the three British soldiers waving them on their way towards Cardiff.

By now Ludwig and Herzler had assumed the lack of lorries was due to the escape being discovered. They knew that heading north for a mile from any point on the A48 near to Bridgend would lead them to the railway line. Still in the built up area of the town, they furtively made their way through the deserted streets. Although there had been no likelihood of a bombing raid in Wales for nearly three years, the two S.S. men benefited from the wartime prudence that maintained a nightly blackout.

Hearing heavy footsteps approaching, Ludwig and Herzler dived over a small garden wall and hid in the shrubs alongside the short path leading to the front door of the house. Both men held their breath as someone turned off the pavement and up the path, stopping within a few feet of the two Germans. What happened next harmed Ludwig's pride more than his escape. Before entering the house, the man chose to relieve himself over the crouching S.S. officer.

Ludwig shook off the indignity and his spirits rose as, within a mile, the men came to the railway line. Better still, within sight was a static freight train. They must have thought their run of bad luck had well and truly ended when the train not only pulled away within minutes of them climbing aboard, but was also, according to their sense of direction, travelling east.

Their elation did not last long. The train could not have covered more than about six or seven miles when it juddered to a halt. Hearing the engine being shut down, and after sneaking a look at the deserted railway siding, the two men decided, once again, to continue their escape on foot. The siding was in the village of Llanharan. With no signposts to help them, Ludwig and Herzler had now hopelessly lost their bearings. Ironically the siding was immediately off the main line, but they decided to walk into the village. Perhaps they may still find a lorry to jump. Very few people tend to walk the streets of Llanharan in the early hours of a Sunday morning. The likelihood was that the only people out and about in the village a couple of hours before dawn on that March day were two S.S. officers and P.C. Philip Baverstock.

By now the breakout had been in full swing for over two hours. Upwards of eighty men had come out of the business end of the tunnel. The escape was well into the realms of what had not been thought possible and the men that were conducting the final checks had taken their chance to flee. As groups of prisoners, grateful to take their chances unaided, were disappearing down the tunnel, nobody spotted that Lieutenant Heinz Tonnsmann was intending to make his way into the night air equipped with a white kit bag.

Tonnsmann crawled out of the tunnel immediately behind Hermann Schallenberg. Poking his head into the cold night air

Tonnsmann watched as the Luftwaffe pilot paused for a brief moment by the copse and then darted to his right. Tonnsmann hauled himself out of the hole, took a deep breath and followed. He got halfway to the woods when he heard a loud English voice yelling the word he recognised as 'stop'. Tonnsmann kept going. A split second before he heard the all too familiar sound of a rifle shot, he felt a searing pain in his shoulder. Still conscious as he lay on the ground he watched helplessly as all hell broke loose.

17. MANHUNT

After his ploughing endeavours, any notion that Garfield Davies may have had of a good night's sleep was put aside when his brother, Jack, woke him at half past four in the morning. Newbridge Farm overlooked the Island Farm camp and although the two men had become used to the orchestrated racket that regularly rolled across the field separating them from the Germans, this particular night surpassed anything that had gone before.

It sounded as if every prisoner was making his own individual contribution to the pandemonium; a distinct combination of singing, shouting and the banging together of metal objects. The brothers soon concluded that there had been an escape – confirmed by the number of guards on the roofs of the easterly huts shining flashlights at a number of men in the Davies' field. Some were crouched motionless; others stood around with their hands above their heads. Jack felt guilty. An hour earlier, on his way home, he had sensed three figures moving stealthily along a hedgerow, but dismissed them as stray dogs.

None of Hermann Schallenberg's Luftwaffe training, or battle experience, could have prevented his involuntary outburst of laughter when, immediately after his friend Tonnsmann had been shot, the assailant disappeared down the hole of the tunnel, amid a string of Anglo-Saxon curses. Other guards were quick to raise the alarm as noisily as possible. Schallenberg, even if he had been capable of making a run towards the woods, thought better of it and stood with his hands raised. A number of his colleagues, still in and around the field, followed suit.

Within minutes, the guards, demonstrating an unusual degree of organisation, had crudely lit the area with handheld torches. A group of them, with dogs, was heading towards the woods. Schallenberg knew that as soon as this inevitable conclusion to the escape eventually happened, a plan was to immediately kick in, to create as much noise as possible throughout the camp. It was working well.

Commander Darling was soon on the scene He took a look at Lieutenant Tonnsmann, writhing in pain on the ground. The wound appeared unlikely to be life-threatening, but nevertheless Darling dispatched one of his men to call an ambulance. Further orders were given to continue searching the woods, while all the prisoners were to be assembled immediately in the parade ground for a roll call.

Meanwhile, in Llanharan, the S.S. officers Ludwig and Herzler, assuming that the alarm had been raised much earlier, now realised the large figure walking towards them was a British policeman. Standing over six feet tall, P.C. Philip Baverstock was a former Welsh Guardsman. He had been the local village bobby long enough to know who had legitimate cause to be walking around his patch in the early hours of any morning. If he did not know them, then it was safe conjecture that they were up to no good. Besides, on seeing him approach, these two men had sidestepped onto a garage forecourt.

Baverstock shone his torch into their faces and demanded to know who they were in his booming voice. The answer caught him by surprise. One of them, using impeccable diction, but with an accent that was unusual to Llanharan, replied. "And who are you?" What should have broken this standoff was that the two highly trained, ruthless, S.S. officers should have overpowered the hapless policeman and made their escape. What actually happened was that Ludwig mistook the large wooden truncheon under Baverstock's coat for a machine gun, and gave himself up. Herzler followed suit and the policeman led his two suspects to the Police Station.

It was not the discovery that the men were escaped POWs that shocked Baverstock: frequent memorandums from his Commanding Officer had warned him that it was only a matter of time before this happened. Instead it was the amount of food and the oddity of their accessories that surprised him. Ludwig and Herzler had certainly ensured an unfair supply of rations. Tins of corned beef, and ample quantities of cigarettes Baverstock could understand: it was the fact that both men carried a pair of bedroom slippers that did not match the policeman's image of the infamous S.S. Putting his bemusement to one side, Baverstock phoned his immediate superior, Inspector James Fitzpatrick.

The senior officer was already on his way to Island Farm. As soon as an ambulance had been summoned to the camp, the Duty Sergeant phoned Fitzpatrick at home. Reports were already coming in of an above average commotion emanating from the prison. Fitzpatrick took the precaution of phoning Superintendent May's home. May agreed that the Inspector had been right to wake him: something out of the ordinary was obviously going on. He asked Fitzpatrick to send a car to pick him up as well. May also gave the order to put all Special and Auxiliary Constables on standby as a precaution. It was now almost five o'clock.

As the two police officers arrived separately at Island Farm they were met by Commander Darling, who briefed them on events. An escape attempt had been nipped in the bud. All fourteen absconding prisoners, who had escaped by a tunnel from one of the eastern perimeter huts, were accounted for. A roll call had been made and all other prisoners had answered to their names. Both policemen spotted the obvious flaw in Darling's counting system but were saved the embarrassment of making it clear to him by the telephone call for the Superintendent from Llanharan Police Station.

Commander Darling was left to conduct a thorough headcount while May began making the phone calls to implement his prized Plan X. He knew that the basis of the painstakingly prepared plan was at least partly superfluous. If two prisoners had appeared on foot in Llanharan, it was conceivable that their more mobile collaborators were already near London.

Lieutenant Rols was indeed out of Wales. His train had emerged from the Severn Tunnel and was now halted near Bristol. Rols and his travelling companion were unaware of how many of their fellow escapees were on the same train, or whether it would eventually move on. If it did, the chances were it would continue due east and they were committed to heading south towards the ports of Southampton and Portsmouth. Besides, if this were Germany, as soon as the escape was discovered any train that had passed through the area would be stopped and thoroughly searched. It was time to change trains.

Meanwhile, Harzheim's hunch that a doctor's car would have a full tank had been sound, although a generous amount of fuel in 1945 was still only enough to cover about fifty miles. The men had gone over their route countless times. From Bridgend the main road would take them to Cardiff. If they could keep on the same road through the city it would continue to Newport and then Chepstow. There the landmark was the River Severn. Forty miles upstream was the English town of Gloucester. Once there, the Castle Bromwich airfield would then be a further sixty miles to the northeast. Having now got a feel for the car he was driving, Harzheim calculated that they had enough petrol to get them to the other side of Chepstow.

They had been driving steadily for about an hour, and judged by the size of the town they were entering, they had reached Cardiff. To avoid what looked ominously like two policemen in the distance they turned off the main road, and a few minutes later were forced to conclude that they were lost. A lone pedestrian was spotted and a quick decision made. They could continue to drive around, wasting petrol and attracting attention, or they could put their English to the test and ask directions.

The man turned out to be a tram driver on his way home. Hans asked him if he knew the way to Gloucester. The man looked blank, so Hans repeated the question. Suddenly the man smiled and repeated the name of their destination, but with two syllables, not three. Harzheim smiled back and apologised for his pronunciation, after all he and his friends were Danes. The pedestrian looked equally pleased: the road these Danish engineers needed to get to took him past his house. He climbed in and directed them towards Newport Road, where he took his leave, assuring the men that by staying on that road they would take the right direction out of Cardiff. By now the Germans had concluded that fate was definitely contriving to get them home.

Superintendent May's instincts told him that he would be searching for considerably more than the fourteen escaped prisoners accounted for at the camp, plus the two now in police care in Llanharan. While Commander Darling and his men, aided by the early morning light, were herding the prisoners through the compound designed for this very purpose, May continued to put his plan into place.

Roadblocks were set up around Bridgend. Neighbouring forces in Cardiff and Swansea were alerted, followed by police divisions in West Wales and England. Every reserve policeman was called in for duty. May's plan employed a network of police officers, some in cars, but most on bicycles, to alert every manned railway site, from mainline stations to remote signal boxes. All trains were to be halted and searched. Extra policemen were dispatched to the primary sabotage targets. Colonel Llewelyn was telephoned at his home at Court Colman and briefed on the events. He told May that he would seek immediate permission to call out his recently disbanded Home Guard.

The Superintendent was concerned to find out, as quickly as possible, if any of the prisoners were armed. Neither the fourteen in custody at the camp, nor the two with P.C. Baverstock, were in possession of anything more threatening than a tin opener. Although the theft from the food store had not yet been discovered, there were no sign of any arms missing from the camp's modest arsenal. May's plan specifically did not call for civilian involvement; however with the fundamental requirement of swift implementation lost, plans needed to be urgently revised.

Commander Darling now completed a methodical head count and the situation was much worse than even May had suspected. Seventy prisoners, in addition to the fourteen caught near to the fence, had got away. Worse news was to follow. An almost apoplectic Colonel Llewelyn was on the phone. He had been refused permission to re-arm his men and was not even to be given petrol supplies to mobilise them. He assured May that the Home Guard would respond in any event. May decided, there and then, to involve the public in the manhunt.

Back at the main police station, the Superintendent called together his most senior officers to assess the situation. None of the fourteen prisoners caught near the camp was very well equipped. However the two held by P.C. Baverstock had enough food to last the best part of a week, along with detailed maps and perfectly adequate compasses. It was probably safe to assume that at least half of the seventy prisoners at large were that well equipped. Freight traffic had been light that evening on the A48, but a number of trains had already passed through the Severn Tunnel. When news arrived that Dr. Baird Milne's car was missing, it did not require a feat of great detection to work out who the thieves had been.

Apart from Jack Davies' belated report of a sighting near to the camp, the only other had been telephoned to the police by William Board, a dairy farmer in the village of Merthyr Mawr, less than half a mile from Island Farm. He had discovered four Germans in one of his milking barns. They had run off in the direction of the warren of sand dunes to the south.

May concluded that most of the escapees were planning to lie low now that it was light, grab some rest and start moving again that night. Search parties should therefore concentrate on the outbuildings of farms and any other places that would provide refuge. Resigning himself to a long day, the Superintendent injected some wry humour into the police station. He asked an assistant to make up seventy map-pins adorned with swastikas. On the large map in the main control room, May carefully placed two pins in Llanharan and put the remaining sixty-eight in a large tin box.

Apart from notifying the B.B.C. in Cardiff of the escape, May had already worked out the most effective way of getting in touch with the Bridgend public. By the time they had finished their breakfasts, every priest, vicar and lay preacher in the area had been visited by one of May's officers. Within a couple of hours an appeal was being made to congregations of every denomination. The messages were clear. Sixty-eight German POWs were on the loose and assistance was required. However, there was no need to panic, as the Germans were not thought to be armed. Above all do not unwittingly give them any help. The advice was to lock up all buildings and immobilise vehicles.

A tank commander always has an accurate grip on how far any amount of fuel will propel him. Sure enough, as Harzheim had predicted, the stolen Austin 10 spluttered to a halt near the village of Blakeney, twelve miles up-river from Chepstow. The four men had at least made it out of Wales. Pushing the car off the road, they discussed what to do next. By now, the Doctor had probably reported his car as stolen, so instead of looking to siphon petrol, it was probably better to steal a new vehicle. It was now fully light and the men were tired and hungry. They realised that they were on the edge of the Forest of Dean, and so it was agreed that they would make camp for the day.

Harzheim and his friends stood a much better chance of a peaceful rest than any of their colleagues still within the ten-mile radius of Bridgend. By mid-morning agnostics were as well briefed as their more devout neighbours and the whole town was gripped by the new sport of 'Hunt the German'. Gangs of children ignored their parents and were searching woods and hills. Almost every farm had a team of workers sticking pitchforks into hay filled barns. On almost every patch of open land there was a team of locals fanning out, armed with an array of farm implements and broom handles.

True to his word, Colonel Llewelyn had somehow managed to mobilise 2,000 Home Guards, albeit mostly on foot. His Porthcawl regiment were better equipped. Throughout the War they were well know as the only Home Guard cavalry troop and were now combing the sand dunes between Ogmore on Sea and their hometown on horseback. Although the responsibility of capturing the POWs remained under the jurisdiction of the police, given the magnitude of the escape, all available Army personnel in the area were seconded to the hunt. By Sunday lunchtime armed guards instructed to inspect every vehicle manned every major road junction. Motorcycle dispatch riders darted between checkpoints. All trains passing through Bridgend were searched thoroughly before they were allowed to depart. A small number of spotter planes from R.A.F. St Athan added an aerial aspect to the drama of the occasion.

It was becoming apparent to everyone that the Germans were well trained in the art of going to ground. By early afternoon only a handful of sightings had been notified to the command centre May had established at Bridgend Police Station. The remains of a campfire had been found in the ruins of Candleston Castle, near to Merthyr Mawr. In addition, a troop of Girl Guides, themselves camping out in woods near Porthcawl, had been asked directions by two prisoners who promptly disappeared.

A couple of boys, caught up in the excitement, and with little sense of danger, were combing Coedymwster woods, near to the village of Coychurch. Nine year-old Gwyn Leyshon pulled at a pair of military boots he saw poking out of a bush. The German soldier wearing them quickly woke up and, along with his partner, ran off, much to the relief of the now terrified children. After the boys notified the local police station an armed detail of soldiers was dispatched to the area. Two hours later there was still no sign of their prey.

By lunchtime, the two S.S. men caught in Llanharan were still the only successes. A rumour began circulating that a U-Boat had been waiting in the Bristol Channel to snatch all seventy back to Germany. Superintendent May did not buy into it, knowing that at this stage of the war a working submarine was far more valuable to Hitler than seventy prisoners. He did, however, begin to fear that the majority of absconders had cleared his area before the escape was discovered.

It was mid-afternoon before the manhunt began to pay off. Elwyn Morris, a farmer in Laleston had been out searching all morning with a group of friends. Returning for lunch, his daughter mentioned a particular sunken copse on the farm, two and a half fields away from the house that she used to use as a den. Elwyn and his neighbour, John Williams, went to the remote location and discovered five Germans asleep amid the remains of a meal. Standing on the raised ground Elwyn shouted to the men to surrender. The POWs woke up, declined Elwyn's offer, and ran off. The farmer, along with his equally unarmed friend, set off in pursuit, frantically waving to a plane that had appeared overhead. The chase lasted a couple of miles before it reached the road that led to the village of Cefn Cribbwr. There, Elwyn continued the hunt while his friend sought assistance. The occupants of a passing bus failed to notice the drama unfolding but by the time the Germans disappeared into a small wood, Army reinforcements had arrived. The five prisoners were quickly rounded up and word sent to a relieved Superintendent May.

The capture sparked a run of luck for the combined authorities. Bill Young was one of the first Special Constables to be pulled out of his bed in Brynna that morning. With a colleague, he had spent a fruitless morning searching barns and haylofts in the area. By three o'clock in the afternoon they were about to call it a day and head for home. Walking along the railway line they saw a blond German soldier strolling aimlessly towards them. He appeared totally lost, could not speak a word of English, and quietly accompanied the reserve officers to Llanharan Police Station. In the meantime, the two prisoners whose sleep had been rudely interrupted by the small boys were caught by an Army patrol in woods near to Coity. They had travelled only a mile.

As three more swastikas were pinned onto Bill May's map, word came in of another four Germans who had been captured near to where Elwyn Morris's already legendary chase had come to an end. P.C. Williams had been on duty most of the previous night. He grabbed a couple of hours rest around lunchtime and signed back on for duty at three o'clock. The R.A.F. station at St Athan was now fully involved in the hunt and all their available officers had been made available. Superintendent May, grateful of the extra help, distributed the R.A.F. men around his local stations, each group being provided with a local constable. P.C. Williams, with his new partner, Flight Lieutenant Swanson, two junior R.A.F. officers and an eager group of local residents set about combing the Llynfi Woods, near to Cefn Cribbwr. It was not long before they came across a group of four prisoners. Again, with no resistance offered, the Germans were taken to the local police station to be collected by one of Commander Darling's lieutenants. The pluckiest apprehension of the day fell to a young A.T.S. woman who had become separated from her search party near to Porthcawl. She spotted one of the Germans and confronted him. Not only did he give himself up immediately, but his friend emerged from the bushes to join him.

Alerted by the report on the B.B.C., a number of Fleet Street editors had dispatched reporters to south Wales. Bill May enjoyed good relationships with the two major Cardiff papers: the morning *Western Mail* and the evening *South Wales Echo*. But like many senior policemen he did not trust national journalists. His use of the local churches, and legwork from his men, had achieved what he had wanted. The public were falling over themselves to help, and presumably would adhere to police requests for extra precautions to be taken, especially at night. Most importantly, there had not been an over abundance of panic. May knew that sensationalism sold newspapers, and was afraid of what these descending hacks would whip up.

The focus of the reporters' attention was the camp itself. Commander Darling was under siege. The press wanted to know exactly how many prisoners had got out. More importantly, how had they done it? One particular journalist, from the *Daily Worker*, enthusiastically latched on to a rumour that the arsenal at the camp had been raided and the 'Nazis' were now armed to the teeth. As the pressure mounted, Darling was forced to release a statement from his superiors at Western Command in Chester, who had consulted with local police regarding the number of prisoners recaptured to date.

It read that "during the night seventy German prisoners, mostly officers' had escaped. Sixteen had now been recaptured, but fifty-four are still at large. Eleven of those who escaped were Luftwaffe officers, a small proportion were naval officers, but the majority were Army officers." Much to the consternation of Colonel Llewelyn, the statement went on to praise the "invaluable assistance" provided by the Home Guard. He was still demanding his men be armed and supplied with petrol.

Pressed by the man from the *Daily Worker*, Western Command released a second statement denying any arms or ammunition had been stolen from the camp. It confirmed that a "thorough check" had been made. The Army also confirmed that the escape had been made using a tunnel. The journalists dashed off to phone their stories to editors, and clear expenses so they could stay on in Wales to cover a story that was far from over.

It was now getting dark and Superintendent May took stock of the situation. He had received a report of one more capture: a lone German wandering wearily through the village of Laleston, carrying an accordion. This brought the total to seventeen. The problem was that, apart from the first two men, whom he now knew to be S.S., none of the prisoners back in captivity were in possession of anything more than basic rations. With the exception of the five who had fled across a couple of miles of field, there had been little resistance. All this made the Superintendent believe that almost all of the committed escapees were still out there. He was confident that if they were still on his patch he would get them. If, however, they had got far enough away before Darling's men had realised they were gone, then it was out of his hands.

A weary Bill May was about to sign off duty when news came in of another two prisoners being picked up. Carl-Heinz Brockmeyer and his group were well clear of the camp by the time that the escape was halted. They sheltered in a quarry and rested until it became dark again. The group included a naval officer, and still being confident of their bearings, they made towards the town of Port Talbot. They knew that there were docks nearby and with a bit of luck there may be a small vessel they could steal.

The deserted streets suddenly became crowded. Brockmeyer spotted the cause; the local cinema had just closed. He and one of his colleagues dived for cover over a wall. By the time the crowds had dispersed the rest of his group had disappeared. As there had been no shouting or shooting, they were probably still nearby. The two Germans carried on in the direction they felt led towards the docks. Here they ran into four Home Guardsmen. Brockmeyer's hopes of saving his family from the Russians were at an end.

18. A Shot in the Dark

Superintendent May had left instructions to be telephoned at home, at any time during the night, with reports of captures. Consequently, when he arrived back at his desk, before light on the Monday morning, he knew the night had drawn a blank. The weather had stayed dry and mild, so escaping prisoners must have been on the move. May was leaning to the conclusion that the majority of them must have already left the area.

As he waited for the newspapers to arrive, his morning tea was made more palatable by the news that three Germans had been caught, without resistance, in a pill box on the outskirts of town. May smiled when he heard that when their captors found them one of the Germans asked if he could finish polishing his shoes before they left. From the moment that the POWs had arrived in Bridgend, he had been impressed by their appearance.

There were now twenty-two swastikas on the map – and forty-eight still in the biscuit tin – when the newspapers arrived at Bridgend Police Station. Bill May read them with mixed feelings. He knew, from many past experiences, that a pack of journalists jumping on a story have the capacity to all make the same mistake. One makes the error, the rest follow, especially when the national papers lack reporters on the ground, and rehash their rivals' stories. When an Army spokesman read out Western Command's first statement the previous evening, it clearly stated that seventy prisoners had escaped and fifty-four were still 'at large'. Commander Darling had provided the figure of seventy after he had made a number of detailed headcounts. It did not include the fourteen that had been captured by the tunnel exit, in the field and nearby woods. They were already locked up. Besides, he had little incentive to make the escape even bigger than it was.

From reports in the morning newspapers, most of the journalists appeared to have added the prisoners caught by the camp guards to the gradually increasing number of escapees apprehended by the police. From paper to paper, this double-counting meant readers were told that around thirty-six POWs were still at large. May saw no reason to correct matters and neither would Commander Darling nor his superiors, he was sure: over twenty-five years of service had bred a degree of cynicism. If, as was looking increasingly likely, some of these prisoners made it back to Germany, May knew that the Army would find a way of fudging the figures to hide their embarrassment.

Of more immediate concern was some reckless reporting. The *Daily Express* coverage was littered with phrases like "Devil-may-care fanatical young Nazis". The *Daily Mirror* was downright incorrect and irresponsible in reporting that four prisoners were known to be armed. Locally, and largely due to the efforts of May's officers, panic had been minimal but these journalists were not helping.

With more and more sightings of escaped prisoners from further afield, much of the responsibility for the manhunt was being taken from May's division and Scotland Yard co-ordinated matters on a national front. Nevertheless Bill May was a perfectionist: his men would continue as if all forty-eight Germans were still on his patch.

At Island Farm, the newspapers did not make pleasant reading for Commander Darling. His camp was described as being rowdy and his guards inept. One reporter must have walked around Island Farm as he wrote that the fence was broken in a number of places. Darling had already made his feelings known to his men, and confined them to barracks until further notice.

Some of the guards took out their anger and frustration on the prisoners. All privileges were withdrawn, which was allowable under the Geneva Convection. Nonetheless, a handful of guards overstepped the line. The senior German officers reported a number of incidents of rough handling. As captured escapees arrived back in camp, a few were pushed into line by a well-placed rifle butt. Karl Ludwig was missing two front teeth. One guard had thought it funny to aim as if to shoot one of the prisoners, firing above his head at the last second.

Commander Darling prided himself on being a professional soldier; he came down heavily on any guard found guilty of the slightest misdemeanour. Darling was fully aware that feelings were running high amongst his men. Almost a year ago to the day there had been an escape by seventy-six Allied prisoners from Stalag Luft III. The breakout, and subsequent manhunt, bore a remarkable similarity to what was now an even bigger escape at Island Farm. Eventually seventy-three of the Allied POWs were captured. Qualified reports had been received, and reported in the press, that the Gestapo cold-bloodedly executed fifty of the recaptured prisoners. The British Government had made it clear that after the war the guilty would be brought to account.

May was also aware of the aftermath of that escape. In his mind it had affected the response of the recaptured Germans. With the exception of those who had got away from Farmer Morris, there had been no resistance, and certainly no violent resistance. He concluded that most of the Germans feared that the British would conduct similar reprisals. May had faith that the authorities would not do so but he was not so sure of some of the more hot-headed citizens on his patch, especially those whose families had suffered losses during the war. For this reason he intended to have words with the writers of some of the more lurid press reports.

Any hope the authorities had of the Welsh weather running to form and flushing out prisoners were dashed soon after dawn, Monday was another fine spring day. Perfect conditions for holing up in woods and forests. All that could be done was to continue the search and hope that luck would favour the hunter.

Fortune was still smiling on Prior, Zielasko, Harzheim and Ehlert, who were unaware they had been spotted abandoning Doctor Milne's car. A local hunt had been triggered but the Forest of Dean terrain lends itself to those seeking to hide. The four men had come across a warm, dry barn and by Monday morning were refreshed after a long rest. A cow, soon to be joined by several others, awakened them. Ehlert joked that its display of affection was undeserved but warranted moving on before the herd's collective interest in them attracted unwelcome attention. The men broke camp and headed northeast.

Back at Bridgend police station the total of swastikas pinned to the map had remained static since early morning. A sighting in Bryntirion, just a mile west of Bridgend, had come to nothing. Scotland Yard was now fully on the case, with roadblocks set up across southern England. All trains arriving at Paddington Station, the London terminus for Wales, were subjected to a thorough search before passengers were allowed to disembark. Commander Darling had received word that a party from the War Office was on its way to Bridgend to hold an enquiry.

For Glenys and Megan Evans the previous twenty-four hours had been terrifying. The two young sisters lived alone at Graig Goch Farm, high on the remote Margam Mountain, to the west of Bridgend. The farm was too inaccessible for electricity, let alone a telephone, and it had been the workers there who had informed the women to watch out for escaped Germans. As dusk descended on Sunday evening, Glenys entered the hallway and her lighted candle illuminated a tall German standing by the front door. She fainted; he quickly left. The sisters decided to leave food outside the house, hoping it would stop the German, or worse still a group of them, re-entering. The plan worked and after a sleepless night the women ventured outside to find the food had gone. They would do the same on Monday night.

That evening saw a small streak of luck for the authorities. Richard Jones, a farmer from the village of Aberkenfig, just north of Bridgend, had been patrolling his land accompanied by an employee, when they came across four Germans crouching in a hedge. They offered no resistance and were taken to the local police station. This success was quickly followed by reports that Special Constables had caught another four P.O.W.s in Pencoed, only four miles from Island Farm. When another Special Constable, Stanley Lewis, apprehended two more prisoners, less than 200 yards from Kenfig Hill Police Station, on the way to Margam, Bill May put the thirty-first and thirty-second swastikas on his map and decided to call it a day.

Just before one a.m. the Superintendent's telephone rang at home. He picked it up, hopeful that more Germans had been captured, but it was bad news. A young woman had been shot and badly wounded in Porthcawl. Details were sketchy but it appeared the shooting was related to the escape. May asked to be kept fully informed.

*

Around an hour previously a shot had rung out in New Road, Porthcawl, an unusual occurrence even during wartime. Arthur Speck, a local gas fitter, was up late with three friends – George Lewis, Frank Jones, and Fred Aston – repairing a broken wireless radio. The four men went into the alleyway which ran along the rear of the houses, but could not see anything. Jones and Aston walked down the lane towards the main road, while Speck and Lewis stayed at their gate.

Out of the darkness a man appeared wearing a Macintosh and waving a torch. He appeared distressed. Speaking in what the men thought was an American accent, he said "Fetch a doctor, I've shot my wife". He led them round the corner of the lane to where a young woman lay, partly propped up by the wall of a garage. She was conscious but bleeding profusely from her stomach and obviously in severe pain. Speck and Lewis could see that beneath his coat the man wore what looked like a Canadian Army uniform. He was still clearly agitated but explained that a German prisoner had accosted them and demanded his coat, and his wife's handbag. The German went to attack the woman and in the ensuing struggle the Canadian had managed to draw his gun and fire: but it was his wife who had been hit. As she fell to the ground the German had run off in the direction of nearby allotments.

Lewis ran off to telephone the police, but they were already on their way. P.C. Thomas Lewis, on duty in the local police station with a reserve constable, had heard the shot. They saw Frank Jones, who was beckoning frantically for them to follow him up the lane to where a badly bleeding woman lay, surrounded by two civilian men and a soldier. Arthur Speck told the policemen that the doctor had been sent for. The soldier kept repeating that he had shot his wife, while the poor woman was crying out in pain.

P.C. Lewis asked the soldier where his gun was. As he went to pull the weapon from his coat pocket the policeman decided to perform the act for him. Asking the men to stay with the woman until the doctor arrived, the two policemen accompanied the soldier to the police station, where Inspector William Matthews, who lived on the premises, had risen to investigate the cause of the commotion.

The soldier was sobbing hysterically, repeating over and over that he had shot his wife. In the warm air of the police station the Inspector could smell drink on his breath. Eventually he told them he was Howard Grossley, a Bombardier in the Canadian Army. P.C. Lewis, anxious to get back to the stricken woman, asked Grossley her name. The question seemed to compose the Canadian. He said, "Lily Griffiths. She's known as my wife." Grossley was put in a cell while P.C. Lewis briefed his superior about how a German had attacked the couple. Lewis was despatched back to the scene while Matthews phoned Superintendent May.

The local doctor, Robert Hodkinson, had arrived quickly on the scene. One look at Lily told him that her wound was very serious. She had been shot in the stomach, with the exit wound worryingly close to her liver. The doctor gave her morphine to relieve the pain and sent one of the men to call for an ambulance. The other three men helped the doctor carry Lily into one of the adjoining houses. Here he noticed several fresh bruises on her face and her legs.

Hodkinson accompanied the woman in the ambulance to Bridgend General Hospital where he conducted a more through examination. The bruises on her face had now swollen and when she was undressed he spotted there were more injuries to arms, legs and lower abdomen. It looked as if she had been held firmly by the arms and kicked several times, with one particularly heavy blow to the stomach. However, it was the gun shot wound that provided the most concern. The bullet had perforated her stomach and the internal bleeding was very serious.

Lily was by now in deep shock and had lost a lot of blood. Transfusions were given and the operating theatre opened. Lily was still conscious and as she was being prepared for surgery the doctor felt it appropriate to tell his patient the seriousness of her injuries. He asked if she could remember what had happened. She told him that her husband had shot her while trying to defend them both against a German prisoner. Hodkinson, an experienced surgeon, performed the operation himself. It was successful insofar as he was able to stem the internal bleeding. The next few days would be critical to his patient's survival.

Meanwhile, Bill May ensured he was kept abreast of events in Porthcawl during the night. The sixth sense of a good policeman told him that something was not right. He gave instructions to Inspector Matthews that on no account were any details of the incident to be given to the press, either by his men or the immediate witnesses. May had hoped that his sleep would have been disturbed by reports of recaptured Germans, not regular updates of an attempted murder.

19. HALFWAY HOME

There had been one success during the night. At about 2 a.m., two policemen patrolling the A48 in the village of Duffryn, about five miles southwest of Cardiff, heard what sounded like a couple of men approaching. The constables hid behind a hedge and apprehended two Germans. Again there was no resistance. While the policemen admired the quality of the map the Germans were carrying, the POWs were quite happy to explain that they were making for Cardiff docks where they planned to jump a ship to Ireland.

As Superintendent May arrived back at Bridgend police station, before dawn once again, reports were coming in of an incident close to the mouth of the Severn railway tunnel, on the Welsh side. Four prisoners had been spotted and a chase ensued among the freight carriages parked in the railway sidings. Two of the Germans were caught; the other pair had escaped.

Other news was also arriving. A stolen motorbike had been found in Monmouth and a local farmer in the Vale of Glamorgan discovered that his cows had already been milked that morning. Details of another two Germans caught during the night in the grounds of Aberpergwm House, near to Glynneath, made that the most westerly capture so far. There were now more swastikas on the map than in the biscuit tin.

For the first time in three days, May had a more pressing priority than the escape. The hospital told him that Lily Griffiths was still in a critical condition but having survived the operation had a chance of recovery. Inspector Matthews gave a full briefing. Grossley was maintaining his story about the escaped prisoner though there had been no other reported sighting. May told Matthews that it was important that the incident remained undisclosed until more information was available. The Inspector said he would have another word with the four witnesses and ask the local residents not to speak to the press.

The Superintendent gave the case to his most senior detective, Inspector Lancelot Bailey. His next task was to contact the Canadian military in London and inform them that one of their men was in police custody in south Wales. The plot thickened further. Bombardier Grossley had been absent without leave for over two weeks.

May then spoke to the handful of reporters that he felt he could trust. He told them that there had been a shooting in Porthcawl but that it was unrelated to the escape. However, given the circumstances that week, he would appreciate the story not being reported until more details were confirmed. In return for their co-operation May promised that they would be the first to receive more detailed information.

Looking through the morning's newspapers, May was concerned to see that two journalists were still being reckless in their reporting. The *Express* was adamant that all the escapees were "rabid Nazis," while the *Chronicle* took the angle that the whole escape was an orchestrated "last fling" sabotage operation, conducted by "fanatical" Nazis. The editors concerned needed to be informed that there was no evidence of sabotage, all captures had been non-violent, there was nothing to suggest that any of the Germans were armed, and only a minority were S.S.

On the other hand, May was forced to smile when reading the *Western Mail* and *Daily Worker*. Colonel Llewelyn had given interviews to the press. The fact that the Home Guard commander had chosen the national paper of Wales was not a surprise; choosing the voice of British socialism was. Llewelyn had made it clear that it was total incompetence on behalf of his superiors not to allow his men to be mobilised immediately after the escape was discovered. After all this was what the police had wanted. The Colonel went on to expand on a theory in respect of the escape that Bill May felt carried considerable merit. The purpose of the mass escape had been to provide distraction in order to allow a few chosen prisoners to get away.

D.I. Bailey arrived at Porthcawl Police Station shortly before 10.30 a.m. and began his investigation. An experienced and well-respected detective, Lance Bailey cut a flamboyant figure within the somewhat staid South Wales Police Force. A gifted amateur thespian, he was well known in his native town of Port Talbot for the extravagant way he played the church organ on a Sunday; flailing arms reaching each end of the elongated keyboard at every opportunity.

Arthur Speck seemed to be the most reliable witness of the four men around when the shooting happened. He had also taken care of Lily until Doctor Hodkinson had arrived. At one stage, Speck reported, while waiting for help to arrive, Grossley had fallen to his knees alongside his stricken girlfriend, crying "My darling! What have I done?" To which Lily replied "Don't worry dear. You couldn't help it." Speck had asked the couple to describe the man who had attacked them. Lily said she did not know. Grossley had merely pointed in the direction of the allotments towards which the German had fled.

More background to the couple came from Ernest Atkinson, and wife Jennie, who owned the guesthouse at 227 New Road. Grossley and Lily had arrived almost two weeks before, on March 3. The family already knew them from their brief holiday there the previous summer. Bailey was also informed that they had a two-year-old son, Anthony, who had not arrived with them this time, but was brought there by Lily a few days later. Mrs Atkinson thought the boy had been staying with Lily's sister in Aberdare. In fact Lily had left him with her sister the previous afternoon in preparation for starting work the next day at the Bridgend munitions factory.

The Atkinsons were shocked to learn that the couple were not married. Jennie told D.I. Bailey that they seemed a happy couple. Ernest, who had a military background having served in the First World War, vouched for Howard Grossley being a good man. He told the Inspector that if he had any doubts they would not have been allowed to stay. His wife then related that before Lily had arrived back from Aberdare that evening, the Atkinsons and Grossley were listening to the 6 o'clock news on the radio, which was still running the story of the escape from Island Farm. Ernie, the Atkinsons' sixteen year-old son, who had become quite friendly with the Canadian, had said that if he had Mr. Grossley's gun than he would go looking for some Germans.

Mr. Atkinson asked Grossley if he possessed a gun, and young Ernie asked if he could see it. Grossley told the boy to go up to his bedroom and bring down a small green bag. The gun was a standard issue Canadian automatic pistol. Like most boys, Ernie was keen to know how the weapon worked. Mr Atkinson was more concerned that the gun was loaded, and told the Canadian to disarm it before he started his demonstration. Grossley obliged, but after showing the boy how the gun could either fire one bullet or repeated shots, reloaded the weapon and put it in the inside pocket of his battledress tunic. Mrs Atkinson asked Grossley if he intended to take the loaded gun out with him. The soldier confirmed he was, adding that he usually carried the weapon. Mr Atkinson suggested that the Canadian go out and "get some German prisoners". Grossley replied that he would use the gun if he saw any.

At about half past six the two men left the house together and made for the Esplanade Hotel on the seafront. By now Grossley had indicated he had another use for the gun. He knew of a U.S. Army sergeant who might buy it from him. Ernest Atkinson only stayed for one pint of beer, leaving Grossley at the bar. The Canadian soon got into conversation with three local men and, in search of Grossley's preferred brand of cigarettes, they all moved on to the Victoria Hotel. They stayed there until the ten o'clock closing time.

Mrs Atkinson had also left the house, soon after the men, to go to the cinema. When she returned, at about ten, Lily was back and sitting in the kitchen knitting a pair of socks for young Anthony. Bailey was keen to know if, at this point, there were any marks on Lily's face. Mrs Atkinson told him there were none. She recounted how Grossley had arrived back about twenty minutes later. Lily had said, "Hello dear, where have you been?" Grossley just merely replied, "out", but then went on to enquire how Anthony was. Mrs. Atkinson could see that Grossley had been drinking, as his cheeks were quite flushed. Grossley then went to go upstairs, motioning his head as if to request Lily to follow him, which she did after finishing her row of knitting. About half an hour later, Mrs. Atkinson heard the couple go out of the front door.

As the Inspector left the Atkinson house he discovered something else about Bombardier Howard Grossley. The soldier wore special silk vests to protect the horrific phosphorous burns that covered his back. None of the family knew how the injuries had been acquired. Bailey had earlier dispatched Detective Sergeant Bill Heap to examine the scene of the shooting. When picking up a Canadian Army tweed cap that Heap had spotted in the front garden of number 183, he noticed a small hole in the front window. The remainder of the pane of glass was intact. Two of the ladies who lived in the house had already found the cause; a bullet was lying on the settee. Lilian Harvey, an employee at the local arsenal, lived in the upstairs room to the front of the house. Both Lilian, and her landlady Lilian Newlyn, had heard a gunshot and a woman's scream just before midnight.

Sergeant Heap was having a productive morning. Not only had he collected two more witnesses, both of whom distinctly remember hearing the scream and shot, he had also tracked down a local taxi driver, William Thomas, who had been drinking with Grossley the night before at the Esplanade Hotel. By the time Thomas had left the Canadian shortly before ten, Grossley had drunk about five pints of beer. In addition, a Frank Rowe, owner of an allotment to the rear of New Road, had approached the policeman. Rowe had found the loaded magazine of a gun.

After discussing these developments with his assistant, Bailey felt it was time to speak to Howard Grossley. The Canadian was calmer than he had been the night before, but his overwhelming concern was to find out about Lily. He confirmed that the cap Sgt. Heap had found was his. Grossley was not a large man, in his mid to late 30s, about 5 feet inches in height, though he appeared bigger due to his stocky build. He wore spectacles, which made him look almost studious. Bailey judged him to be mild mannered, courteous and articulate. He told Grossley that he would have to remain in custody while enquiries continued as there were points in his statement that were unclear. He was to be transferred to Bridgend Police Station. In answer to his request, it would not be possible at this stage for him to see Lily.

Later that afternoon, Bailey discussed the case with his superior, Bill May. The positioning of the bullet in the front room of the house did not add up with the direction that Grossley claimed the German ran immediately after the struggle. More information had come to light about the Canadian soldier. Catherine Davies, Lily's married sister had made the arduous bus ride down from Aberdare. Grossley had recently admitted to her that he had a wife living in America.

Bill May had expected the Canadian Army to intervene by this stage. It was commonplace for Allied authorities, in such situations, to take the suspect into military care. May would have resisted: he felt strongly that war should make no difference to the investigation of criminal acts. However, in Grossley's case, the Canadians seemed happy to let the matter be handled by South Wales Police. One other thing did not make sense to May and Bailey: if Grossley had suffered such serious burns, why had he not been repatriated?

*

Two more German prisoners were captured that morning. When Glenys and Megan Evans' brother heard how terrified the women had been, he decided on a pragmatic way to flush the prisoners off Margam Mountain. He set fire to it. The plan seemed to have worked, when, on Wednesday morning, with the higher gorse land still burning, farmhands on Eglwys Nunydd Farm, on the lower slopes near to Margam Park found signs of someone having slept in a hayrick.

There followed a full-scale hunt throughout the neighbouring farms. A posse of farm workers, some armed with pikes and billhooks and one carrying a twelve-bore shotgun, made sweeps of the land, working upwards from the local Post Office. Sure enough, two Germans were spotted and eventually trapped between two groups of labourers. Any notion the prisoners may have had of making a run was reconsidered when a couple of rounds of shot sailed over their heads.

The captives were taken in a dray back to Eglwys Nunydd Farm, and a telephone. The lady of the farm, Nancy Thomas, made the two guests welcome with cups of tea, while everyone waited for the police to arrive. One of the prisoners, a man in his forties, was most grateful. The younger man, more fitting the newspaper stereotype Nazi fanatic, sneered and made a gesture of throwing away his cup of tea. A couple of the farm hands took him into a nearby barn to deliver a lesson in etiquette.

It was not until early evening that the two latest swastikas were added to May's map, and again the drama unfolded on the hills to the north of Port Talbot. Elizabeth Davies was baking in the kitchen of her farm, when a dishevelled and exhausted man knocked on her door and asked directions to Swansea. He spoke very good English, but with a strong guttural accent. She invited him in for tea and cakes, and although he seemed very tempted, he pointed out that he had two friends outside. Mrs Davies extended her invitation. As the three men tucked into the home cooking she told her son, in Welsh, to get help.

When a group of locals duly arrived, none of the Germans seemed to have the strength to make another escape. The Davies family took the opportunity to share a meal with them until the transport arrived back to Island Farm. One of the prisoners told them how he had hoped to be a regional governor after a successful German invasion. He joked that if Germany eventually won the war he would ask to be put in charge of Wales

Later that evening a bus, with three miners aboard, was making its way towards Glynneath. The driver, Gwyn Lewis, who also worked as a special constable, saw four suspicious-looking men creeping along a hedgerow. He shouted to his passengers what he wanted them to do and as the bus pulled up the three miners jumped out and grabbed one suspect apiece. Gwyn Lewis gave chase to the fourth, but he got away. He was found about an hour later. A policeman had spotted him riding between two wagons on a freight train and contacted the next station along the line. The German was still in position when the train pulled in. Resigned to his fate, the prisoner asked if he was in Cardiff.

The night yielded up a further three captives. Gordon Prosser, a Detective Sergeant in Cardiff, was driving through the well-to-do neighbourhood of Cyncoed, which had recently suffered a spate of burglaries. He spotted what he thought to be a tramp and pulled his car over to speak to the man. When his first few questions drew nothing but a blank expression, the Sergeant tried a different line of inquiry. Falling back on the German he had learnt while serving there immediately after the Great War, he asked the man if he was an escaped prisoner from Island Farm. The answer was 'jawohl'. Prosser took the German to Cardiff police station and gave him tea and sandwiches before handing him over.

On the Welsh border the two Germans who had escaped capture at the mouth of the Severn Tunnel were caught separately, within an hour of each other. One was found hiding in a static freight car by a railwayman, the other caught nearby by a policeman. The tally was now a round fifty.

When Bill May called a meeting of his officers, early on Wednesday morning, it was to review the overall situation. Although Bridgend remained the police command centre, liaising between other forces, there had not been a prisoner caught in that Division since Monday. Nevertheless, May stressed that although it was looking increasingly unlikely that the twenty prisoners who had so far evaded capture were still on their patch, all the roadblocks and searches must be maintained. The orders were not received with enthusiasm as heavy rain had now set in across south Wales. What had been an extraordinary week was about to take a tragic twist: word came from the hospital that Lily Griffiths was dying.

20. THE CANTERBURY THREE

Lily Griffiths was twenty-nine years old. Lying in a private room in Bridgend General Hospital, the bruising now completely hid her natural good looks. Her left eye was almost closed and a purple patch covered the lower half of her face. In addition there were several marks on both her arms and her wrists which testified to her having been tightly gripped. The nurses agreed with Dr. Hodkinson's initial thoughts; the large bruise, starting on her stomach and continuing down to her groin, must have been caused by a vicious kick. Apart from a week-old mark on her left arm, all the injuries were fresh.

But the beating was not a fatal one. It was the damage caused by the bullet that would kill her. It had entered through her left breast, passing through one of her lungs, stomach and liver before exiting out of her right side. Dr. Hodkinson had feared that the injuries would continue to bleed internally and when he examined her on Wednesday morning he could see straight away that her damaged lung had collapsed. He decided another operation was needed, but was not hopeful that it would save her. The medical staff were now also aware of Lily's other condition: she was three months pregnant.

At the police station, Lance Bailey had decided it was time for a further interrogation of Bombardier Grossley. The detective wanted to clear up some anomalies in his version of events. Grossley's statement claimed two Germans had attacked him and Lily. This matched what he had told Thomas Lewis, one of the men who had arrived on the scene soon after the shot was fired. However, according to Lewis's friend Arthur Speck, Grossley had indicated to him that it was only one man who had run off towards the allotments. Bailey raised the discrepancy with Grossley and told him he was puzzled that there had been no other sightings, before or after, of any escaped POWs in the area.

Grossley was defiant: "I still say we were attacked by Germans."

Bailey pursued a separate line. "Do you know in which direction you fired your automatic?" he asked.

Grossley was again adamant. "Yes. I fired at them down the alley-way."

It was game, set and match to the Inspector. Confronted with the evidence that showed that the one and only bullet fired from his pistol had ended up in the front room of the house on New Road, Grossley cracked, saying that he must have been crazy to have made up the story about the Germans. He had wanted to tell the truth from the start. The Canadian now told Bailey exactly what had happened.

Back at the hospital things took a turn for the worse. As soon as the doctor cut open Lily's chest he knew there was no hope for her. He drained two pints of blood from her chest cavity, but, by now, the whole area was hopelessly infected. As Lily lay on the operating table her baby was aborted.

One advantage of using gas and air to anaesthetise a patient is a short recovery period. When Lily asked to know how she was, Dr Hodkinson told her the truth: she was going to die. Having been involved in the case from the start the doctor knew, under the circumstances, there were important legal requirements to go through.

By the time Hodkinson had contacted Bailey, Howard Grossley had been formally charged with the attempted murder of Lily Griffiths and had the assistance of a local solicitor, George Sibbering-Jones. Bailey knew that Lily's statement effectively absolved Grossley, and from what Hodkinson had just told him, there was very little time to collect the one piece of evidence he still needed.

At a quarter past eleven that night, a group of men entered Lily's hospital room. She was still conscious and, considering the seriousness of her condition, remarkably lucid. She knew her doctor but did not recognise D.I. Bailey, the solicitor, or the two Justices of the Peace that made up the sombre-looking party. Her eyes were on the soldier standing at the back of the group. "Howard, do you know I'm dying?" she said. Grossley didn't answer. He had been given strict instructions that if he spoke to his girlfriend he would be removed from the room.

Lancelot Bailey explained who he was and why everybody was there. After he had finished, Lily confirmed that she understood. Dr Hodkinson nodded to the policeman, indicating that he was happy for the process to continue. Lily was sentient and knew what was happening. Henry Williams, Bridgend's senior magistrate, then asked her to swear an oath in respect of anything she may say.

The Inspector read Lily's original statement to her, in which she claimed that Grossley had accidentally shot her while trying to defend them both against an attack. When Bailey had finished reading the document he asked Lily if she had anything to add.

Struggling with the severe pain, Lily spoke in a weak voice. "I don't wish to add anything." She paused for breath before continuing. "Only that Howard would never hurt me." She stopped again before finishing what she wanted to say. "He's always been good to me."

There was silence in the room before Grossley's lawyer told Lily that his client had made a statement to the police, telling them what had really happened in Porthcawl on Monday night. Lily could see from Grossley's face that it was time to tell the truth. She began to cry, saying that she could not stand it, but eventually composed herself and began speaking, each short statement being interrupted by a long, breathless pause.

"He wasn't sober on the night I was hurt... He said he was going to do away with himself ... to make it easier for me... He put his hand inside his blouse and took out a revolver... I tried to take it off him and there was a sharp report and I felt hurt... The revolver went off when we were struggling... I tried to take it from him and it was then that I heard the report and felt the pain."

She could not say anymore. Henry Williams had carefully written down everything she had said. He read it back to her and asked her to sign the deposition. Lily could barely raise her hand, but managed to put her usual neat signature at the end of the document. The men left, Grossley included. This was the second time that both Grossley's and Lily's statements matched. The difference this time was that Lance Bailey believed them.

★

As the drama unfolded in the hospital, life at Island Farm was slowly returning to normal. The prisoners brought back to the camp after capture were initially held in the camp theatre, and fed punishment rations. Carl-Heinz Brockmeyer, whose spirits were probably lower than most, went back into character and raised the others by knocking out singalong tunes on the battered, out of tune, piano.

If Commander Darling wanted to keep his spirits up he should have avoided reading the newspapers, which now turned their attention to how the escape had happened. Many voiced criticism of the lax guarding. There were calls for the Home Guard to take over in all POW camps. The leader column in the *South Wales Echo* picked up on how the German prisoners had, since the opening of the camp, maintained a physiological advantage over their guards. A forty-five foot tunnel is not "scratched out" in days, it said. An immediate and full inquiry by the War Office was required. Darling did not need to be reminded that an inquiry had already been convened and was due to start the following day.

A lone newspaper quoted, inaccurately, that the local police still felt the remaining POWs escapees were hiding in the vicinity of Bridgend. Most of the press took the view that the more determined escapees were now scattered across southern Britain, and some, more than likely, had already made it out of the country. The previous inaccuracies in respect of numbers, were now mostly corrected. Depending on their sources, and time of going to press, the papers stated that around twenty prisoners were still loose on Wednesday night.

There had not been a capture all day. Reports arriving at Bridgend Police Station put escapees even further afield. There were two confirmed sightings of three escaped prisoners in Kent. Apparently the men had entered a café in Surrey Road, Canterbury. One spoke impeccable English, the others remained silent. When they realised that they were attracting unwanted attention the men left, driving off in a lorry.

To the collective authorities in Bridgend, this was the most disturbing news so far. Kent was littered with airfields, and around the coast there were plenty of harbours full of small boats capable of making the short journey across the English Channel. In the prevailing chaos of Western Europe, as the Allied forces advanced towards Berlin, a group of men capable of getting this far could easily disappear on the continent.

It was midnight on Wednesday before a fresh capture took place. Richard Davies had spent a nervous week at work, the sole operator of a remote signal box at a railway junction near to the small town of Cwmavon, north of Port Talbot. He heard someone climbing the steps to his box and hoped it was one of the local policemen who had made a point of calling in frequently since the escape.

His visitor was a German POW, who on entering the warm room immediately raised his hands above his head. The man was soaking wet, and looked desperately tired and hungry. Signalman Davies made him welcome, sharing his packed supper of Spam sandwiches and drying the German's clothes on the heater. Neither man spoke the other's language although the Welshman made light of the occasion by saying with a smile, "Heil Hitler!" The German shook his head mournfully and said "Nein." When a policeman arrived to make the regular check, he also sat down for a cup of tea before taking away the refreshed, and grateful, German.

Two hours later P.C. William Williams was on duty patrolling the grounds of a small munitions factory in Lily Griffiths' hometown of Aberdare. The officer saw three figures in the distance whom he called to stop. They ignored his first request but not his more forceful second. It was inconceivable to most of the escaping prisoners that policemen were unarmed. The three Germans gave themselves up. P.C. Williams was impressed with some of the medals they were carrying. Two of them had been decorated with the Iron Cross, one first class.

Lieutenant Sund Rols and the sergeant accompanying him had reached their next goal, the south coast of England. After changing trains near Bristol early on Sunday morning, they had boarded another goods train heading south that had also come from south Wales, and was destined for the town of Eastleigh in Hampshire. The train had been searched as it left Wales, so the men enjoyed an unhindered journey. After discovering where they were they realised that the large port of Southampton was only a few miles distant. The freight wagon in which they were riding had been parked in a seemingly deserted goods yard. Rols decided that they would make camp there. Their hideout appeared safe enough and they could take their time to properly reconnoitre the local coastline.

At about six o'clock on Thursday morning a railway shunter arrived to move some of the freight wagons. Seeing what seemed to be a man in German uniform disappearing behind one of the vehicles, he alerted the police. Within minutes the area was cordoned off and a full-scale hunt was taking place. Rols realised he had been spotted and, panicking, the two men broke cover, leaving their kitbags and provisions. Meanwhile, the police had sent for their secret weapon, Mrs. Nina Elms and her bloodhounds. She had recently helped the Hampshire police catch a murder suspect on the run and the present search was soon over when the two Germans were found hiding in a cement truck.

As Rols' luck was coming to an end, Werner Zielasko was joking that it was almost like being on holiday. With his three companions he had made a comfortable camp in a small wooded valley next to a stream. It was Oswald Prior's turn to clean the fire. Hans Harzheim had even ventured into a nearby village and returned with a newspaper. The men laughed as they realised they were amongst the twenty Island Farm prisoners still reported as missing. They speculated on which of their colleagues were still in with a chance of getting clean away. The other headlines did not make such pleasant reading. Allied troops now occupied the Ruhr and, more worryingly, the dreaded Red Army was within forty miles of Berlin.

The escapees had worked out that they were less than a mile from the large airfield at Castle Bromwich, near Birmingham. Progress from the Forest of Dean had been slow and steady; a combination of night marches and the occasional short hop on a freight train. Steffi Ehlert had spent the morning staring into the sky observing what type of planes were landing and taking off. Most were small twin-engine craft. He assured his colleagues that he could fly whatever they could steal. The plan was to wait until dark to make a reconnaissance of the airfield. If the opportunity presented itself there and then they would make their move. The group knew they had led a charmed existence since getting out of the tunnel and prayed that their luck would hold for this final leg. It didn't. Steffi was the first to hear them. A farmer had followed Harzheim from the paper shop and now returned with his shotgun and two special constables. The adventure was over.

Later that afternoon, as the swastika tally in Bill May's office showed sixty on the map and ten in the biscuit tin, Edward Williams, the Member of Parliament for Glamorgan and Ogmore, stood up in the House of Commons. He directed an innocuous question to Arthur Henderson, the Financial Secretary of the War Office: "Does the Secretary of State have any statement to make about the escape of prisoners of war from the camp at Bridgend, Glamorgan?"

The Minister had prepared his answer. He began, "An escape of sixty-seven German prisoners of war, of whom sixty-five were officers, took place at 04.00 hours on March 11 from a camp in South Wales. Forty-eight of them have now been recaptured." Henderson went on confirm that the tunnel was twenty yards long with an eighteen-inch square entrance. He concluded by saying that a court of inquiry was being convened, to be held in camera.

The local MP asked whether or not the forthcoming enquiry would look at the question of where the camp was sited. The answer was negative. The Secretary of State had said all he wanted to say. Four supplementary questions from more quizzical Members, asking for further details, were brushed away by saying that the answers would be a matter for the forthcoming inquiry to look into.

The Minister's statement caused confusion at Bridgend Police Statement. The discrepancy regarding the number of escapees caught to date was easy to explain; perhaps the Ministry had not been briefed on all of the most recent captures that day. It was the reduction of the figure that had escaped the previous Sunday, by three, that was difficult to comprehend. Western Command had issued the figure of seventy after several headcounts that day. The Police were fully aware that the Army had, for obvious reasons, not included the fourteen POWs that had been caught quickly in the immediate vicinity of the tunnel. Calculating how many of your prisoners have escaped is a relatively straightforward task for any gaoler with the time and conditions to conduct accurate headcounts. Western Command, at no stage over the next four days, had seen fit to adjust the figure downwards, and they would have had good motive to do so as soon as they had found any error. After all, sixty-seven is marginally less embarrassing than a round seventy. The cynics at Bridgend Police Station were quick to link this sudden reduction in numbers to the sighting of three prisoners tantalisingly close to skipping from Kent to the continent. Bill May was philosophical. If there were now three less Germans to catch, so be it.

Such conjecture was of no interest to Lance Bailey. Lily Griffiths was still alive but fading slowly away. Her sister Catherine had been at her bedside for most of the week. Late on Thursday afternoon she arrived at Bridgend Police Station asking for the Inspector. Lily had said something to her that she felt the police should know about. On hearing this new information, and realising that Lily only had hours to live, Bailey, accompanied by Sergeant Heap, rushed to the hospital. Lily was still conscious, but very weak. A nurse, Beryl Edwards, was in attendance. Bailey asked Lily how she was. She told him she was dying. The Inspector asked her if she wanted to tell him what she had told her sister. She did. As Lily began speaking, Bailey diligently wrote down her words on a sheet of foolscap paper.

The dying woman stated that when Grossley had returned to the guesthouse on the Monday night, and they were in the bedroom, he had started beating her. Lily was determined she would no longer put up with it. Grossley made her put on her coat and walk up the road with him. Here he continued to beat her. Lily asked him to "be decent" but Grossley would not listen. She told him that if he altered his ways then "things will change". As she told him that she would speak to him when he was sober, he pulled the gun out of his pocket, saying "You have turned against me now". With the gun in his hand he said "I will finish it off now". A shot was fired and Lily told Grossley she had been hit. He said he was sorry. As Inspector Bailey was still writing, Lily added, "He has treated me terribly the last three years." Bailey read back what he had written; Lily signed the piece of paper. The Inspector, Sergeant Heap and Nurse Edwards signed as witnesses. Lily had one more thing to say: "That is the God's honest truth."

The two policemen left. Lily remained conscious until five o'clock the following morning. Half an hour later she died. When word reached Inspector Bailey he called Howard Grossley's lawyer and asked him to attend the Police Station. The Canadian was charged once again, this time with murder.

Four of the remaining seven prisoners were caught in the early hours of Friday morning. While some of their colleagues had travelled as far as Hampshire, Warwickshire and Kent, this group was still within twenty miles of Island Farm. William Griffiths was sitting in front of the fire in his home at Cymmer, near Port Talbot, having just finished his shift in the local colliery. Hearing footsteps outside, he looked and saw four men disappearing into the shadows. He called the police and they were soon on the trail of the men.

Realising they were being chased, the Germans left the mountain track they were following. Unknown to them, this decision put them in serious danger as they were heading towards a treacherous bog. The police inspector leading the chase called out to them, frantically waving his torch, and the men halted within a few yards of the darkened quagmire. Like so many of their peers they appeared relieved that their escapade was over.

Almost every form of top-flight sport had been affected by the War. Many careers were lost as the war years clashed with the peak of a sportsman's prowess. John Hopkins was on the verge of a Welsh rugby cap when war broke out. Once a promising wing, at thirty-two he knew that his opportunity of dashing down the touchline at Cardiff Arms Park had been and gone. Nevertheless Hopkins still had a turn of speed, which came in useful on the Saturday afternoon as he found himself chasing three German prisoners over his field.

Cwmcyrnach Farm lay on the edge of the village of Glais, near to Swansea. Hopkins's wife and mother had become suspicious of the three men when they could not understand the answer to their greeting as they passed in the lane. The men took off and Hopkins was soon in pursuit. After almost a week of sleeping rough it was a one-sided race. Like so many before them, when caught they gave up without a struggle. Hopkins, who had spent a period with both the

Leicester and Glamorgan police forces before coming home to run the family farm, knew exactly what to do. He took his prisoners to the local post office and phoned for help. The Germans gratefully accepted the Postmistress' offer of tea. When the police arrived John Hopkins was still smiling at how one of the Germans had described the whole adventure. It had been "good sport".

At Bridgend Police Station it had been an extraordinary and gruelling six days. When the call came through from Swansea, three more swastikas went up on the map to a big cheer. There were, however, still three remaining in the biscuit tin.

21. SAFE CONVICTION?

The inquiry, hastily convened in Bridgend, found that a number of factors had contributed to the escape at Camp 198. Poor lighting, lack of roll calls, inadequate policing of the camp – especially the gardening area where much of the tunnel dirt had been disposed – and the absence of loose guard dogs outside of the perimeter fence were blamed. It was discovered that many of the tools used to dig the tunnel had been left lying around by the workers upgrading the camp ready for the influx of high security prisoners. These findings were fed into the wider inquiry being held at Government level. The files were then destroyed.

Commander Darling was broadly exonerated; after all he had spent the previous four months unsuccessfully asking for resources that would have reduced the now obvious defects. Within weeks of the escape he was promoted to Inspector of Prison Camps for the whole of Western Command and would go on to play an important role immediately after the war helping repatriate German POWs. The Army formally thanked the police for their role in the manhunt and Superintendent May received a letter of commendation from his Chief Constable who asked for his gratitude to be passed on to the Home Guard, Air Raid Wardens and the local clergy. The public, who according to the Chief Constable, had "fulfilled all expectations", got back to daily life after all the excitement and Bridgend returned to what passed as normal in the last months of the war.

Many of the remedies recommended by the inquiry were impossible to implement in the short term and the decision was taken to close Island Farm and distribute the prisoners to other camps. As dawn broke on Easter Saturday, three weeks after the breakout, the 1,600 German prisoners were escorted from the camp to the railway station. Their marching was as impeccable and the singing as loud as the day they arrived.

In Europe the war was grinding into its final phase. With the Rhine breached there was no natural barrier west of Berlin and in the east the Red Army was closing on the German capital. Within days of the first Allied troops arriving on the eastern bank of Rhine, the German Commander-in-Chief received the call he had been expecting, summoning him to Hitler's new headquarters in a bunker underneath the Chancellery building.

In the privacy of the High Command mess, General von Rundstedt was well known for his impression of Hitler, mimicking the Fuhrer's way of triumphantly entering a room, chest pushed out, arms moving vigorously across his body and his head disdainfully turning from side to side. This time the General found a much different figure. Hitler resembled an old man; as he shuffled into the room his arms and body trembled violently.

There was none of the usual lambasting and screamed utterances of blame for allowing the Allies to make their crucial breakthrough. Instead Hitler thanked von Rundstedt for his loyalty and formally presented him with the Swords to the Knight's Cross. He told the General that he would be saved from the annoyance of flying courts martial, which could issue summary death penalties. He knew von Rundstedt would not want to participate in "such a bloodbath". The General was finally to be allowed to step down, with immediate effect.

Von Rundstedt, accompanied by his ever-present batman and his son, who had been serving on his staff for three years, was driven to the family home at Kassel where Bila, the General's wife joined the party. For nearly two months they moved desperately around Germany in search of sanctuary from the approaching Allied armies. These weeks on the road took a toll on von Rundstedt and it was decided to head for the spa town of Bad Tolz.

As the elderly General recuperated in what had been one of Germany's most exclusive sanatoriums, American troops were closing on the town. An S.S. panzer division held the 36th Texas Division at bay for nearly two days. On 1 May Lieutenant Joseph Burke entered the sanatorium to find Germany's most respected officer sitting with his son in front of a log fire. Von Rundstedt slowly raised himself onto his arthritic leg and addressed the American officer, saying, "it is a most disgraceful situation for a soldier to give himself up without resistance". Hitler's favourite General was taken into captivity.

A further twist was in store during the dying days of the war in Europe. On 12 April President Roosevelt died at his home. Battle-hardened American troops wept openly. The Japanese claimed it was suicide, while Josef Goebbels hailed Roosevelt's death as "the turning point". In the meantime, Hitler had issued a directive that any officer giving an order to retreat was to be summarily shot. Presumably this was the type of indignity he had spared von Rundstedt. The Fuhrer maintained to all around him that within weeks he would have his hands on hundreds of jet bombers, along with a new type of V Rocket and an atomic bomb. All of these weapons had actually been at varying stages of development but Allied advancement and systematic air strikes had destroyed their construction.

Heinrich Himmler, now in command of the western armies, was the first Nazi leader to break rank, offering surrender to the western powers, but not to Russia. Churchill held firm, saying surrender to the Allies must be total and unconditional. Three days afterwards, American and Russian troops met on the banks of the River Elbe. Both armies had now seen the full horror of Nazi atrocities as the concentration camps at Belsen, Auschwitz and Dachau were liberated. Two of the German Generals implicated in the bomb plot of 1944 were amongst the near-dead at Dachau. Thousands of Allied POWS were being freed everyday, many at the point of death after being starved for months. In Italy, on 28 April, Mussolini was captured and shot by partisans.

On 30 April a single shot rang out that signified the end of the Nazi dream. As Russian soldiers waved the Red Flag from the windows of the Reichstag, less than a mile away Adolf Hitler shot himself. The war in Europe would stagger on for another eight days. Many pockets of German resistance held out to the last man. A bigger concern now to Churchill was how far the Russians would advance westwards. British troops were positioned to prevent any Soviet move into Denmark. Hostilities officially came to an end with the signing of a series of surrenders, all coming into effect at one minute to midnight on 8 May. Within hours impromptu street parties were breaking out all over Britain.

It would take another four months for the war in the Far East to end. By this stage, the Japanese demonstrated an apparent willingness to be slaughtered defending hopeless positions, while an American soldier could expect to survive, on average, three weeks before becoming a casualty. After 70,000 Japanese troops were killed defending the island of Okinawa, the Japanese Emperor Hirohito accepted that defeat was inevitable and instructed his ministers and military chiefs to make all possible attempts to end the war by diplomatic means. Unfortunately, the Japanese would not accept unconditional surrender, and the Americans would not stop short of anything less.

On 17 July, Roosevelt's successor, President Harry Truman, met

Winston Churchill and Joseph Stalin for the first time at a summit in the German town of Potsdam, twenty miles outside the ruins of Berlin. The mistakes of Versailles were not to be repeated, but the depth of the rifts over the future of eastern Europe were now apparent. Stalin was assuming control of Poland, and had initiated the establishment of a Communist government in Yugoslavia. There were other developments among the Allies. Truman had brought news of the successful testing of the first atomic bomb in the New Mexico desert the day before. Politically, Churchill did not survive the sixteen-day conference, returning to London midway through for the results of a General Election. The British people had decided to replace their wartime leader and it was the new Labour Prime Minister, Clement Atlee, who returned to Potsdam as the senior British representative.

Russia had not been at war with Japan during the conflict, but Stalin insisted, to the chagrin of his wartime partners, that his country share in any forthcoming occupation. Ninety per cent of the Japanese navy had been destroyed, the air force was crippled and industry decimated by American bombing. Nevertheless the decision was made to drop an atomic bomb on the city of Hiroshima on the morning of 6 August, killing an estimated 80,000 people instantly. Two days later Russia declared war on Japan.

The Americans had planned to drop a second bomb, five days later, if Japan did not surrender immediately. With bad weather forecast the operation was brought forward two days. The target was Kokura but cloud cover meant the bomber diverted to the secondary target of Nagasaki. This time 40,000 perished. Emperor Hirohito, on hearing the news, immediately instructed his government to "bear the unbearable" and on 2 September, representatives of Japan boarded the U.S. battleship *Missouri*, anchored in Tokyo Bay, to sign the formal instrument of surrender. Six years and one day after it had started, World War Two was over.

★

Howard Grossley had been born in Canada but brought up by a foster family in the U.S. state of Vermont. When he was seventeen he married a local girl, Marie. She was a year younger than him and pregnant. The couple never lived together as man and wife and when the baby was born it was Marie's parents who brought up the boy. She moved away to work as a maid on a large estate. Grossley had volunteered to join the Canadian Army in July 1940 and arrived in Britain on 5 September that year.

Lily Griffiths had already moved away from Aberdare to London where she had another sister. It was in the capital that she had met Grossley. Although she kept the relationship a secret from her family in Wales, she had been living with him since before their son was born. Grossley had been claiming an allowance for his wife and son in America but around the time that Lily was due to give birth he asked his superiors to check that the money was being received and asked to claim a separate allowance for Lily and their child. After looking into the matter the Canadian authorities concluded that Grossley, being estranged from his wife, had not been entitled to a married man's allowance and any money claimed would have to be clawed back from his pay. In addition his claim for Lily was turned down. It transpired that Grossley had been trying, unsuccessfully, for a number of years to get his wife to agree to a divorce. The following two years had been very difficult financially for Grossley and Lily, who had to work while not in the best of health. Just prior to his going Absent Without Leave Grossley's application to leave the Canadian Army, in order for him to take up a civilian job offer, was turned down.

It was inevitable that a deserter would not receive much sympathy in a British court in the immediate aftermath of the war in Europe, and with troops still dying in the Far East. On Wednesday 11 July 1945, Bombardier Howard Grossley appeared before Mr. Justice Singleton at Swansea Crown Court, charged with the murder of Lily Griffiths. He pleaded not guilty.

Unknown to the jury, the defence lawyers had already successfully argued to the Judge that the statement Lily made to Inspector Bailey hours before she died was not legally admissible evidence. There had been no magistrate present at the time and the words "I will finish it off now then" were vague. Did they mean Grossley was intending to finish off himself or Lily?

The court heard from the arresting officers, the landlady Mrs Atkinson, and several witnesses in the vicinity of the shooting. Dr Hodkinson gave evidence, as did the two nurses at Bridgend hospital who had witnessed Lily's deathbed statements. Dr Jethro Gough, who had performed the subsequent post mortem, confirmed that the cause of death had been a septic chest infection resulting from a bullet wound. The prosecuting barrister, Mr. Ralph Sutton K.C., placed great emphasis on Dr Gough's evidence that Lily's body also showed extensive bruising. Detective Inspector Bailey was called, and Lily's statements were read to the court.

The prosecution also relied heavily on the evidence of two ballistic experts. Francis Morton worked for the gun manufacturer Webley Scott and had thirty-four years experience of handling firearms. He had inspected Grossley's gun and found that in spite of the weapon being forty years old it was in relatively good condition. Morton was asked to explain how the firing mechanism worked and stated that firing the Colt revolver required two pulls on the trigger, the second needing to be at a pressure of six pounds. In answer to the prosecution, Morton confirmed that it was impossible for the gun to go off without a deliberate pull of the trigger. The next expert witness, George Carter, a staff chemist at the police forensic laboratory at Cardiff, had studied the clothing Lily had been wearing on the fateful night. He had found a bullet hole consistent with her injury, but there were no signs of scorch marks on her coat, blouse or underwear. Carter had then conducted tests on Grossley's revolver, using similar ammunition, and found that for burn powder marks to appear the target needed to be no further than sixteen inches away from the gun when it was fired.

The prosecution case closed halfway through the second morning of the trial. Mr. Glyn-Jones K.C., acting for Grossley, informed the court that he did not intend to call any witnesses and that the defendant would not be giving evidence, relying instead on his sworn witness statements. This left both Counsels to make their closing submissions. Mr. Sutton reminded the jury of the bruises on Lily's body that could only have been caused by Grossley and that the defendant had initially made a false statement, trying to blame the shooting on escaping German prisoners of war. Although not strictly relevant to the circumstances surrounding Lily's death, Mr Sutton slipped in the fact that throughout the time Grossley was living with Lily he had a wife in the United States. The testimony of the expert witnesses made clear that the gun had been deliberately fired, and from a distance. This was a clear case of premeditated murder.

Mr. Glyn-Jones rose to make a final attempt to save Grossley's life. To be guilty of murder the jury needed to be satisfied, beyond reasonable doubt, that this was not a tragic accident. Although the court had heard considerable evidence from several witnesses, one crucial fact could not be clearer. The second statements of both the defendant and the victim were, in substance, the same story. However, there had been no collusion between them since the night of the shooting. Lily knew she was dying. What better motive was there to tell the truth? The case of the defence was simple. There were simply no grounds for either murder or indeed manslaughter.

It was left to Judge Singleton to sum up the case to the jury before it retired to decide on the verdict. His words were far from helpful to Grossley's case. The jury returned the same afternoon after finding the Canadian guilty of murder. Grossley paled visibly as he was sentenced to hang.

The defence immediately filed an appeal, despite the judge refusing to grant leave for such a measure. Grossley was returned to Cardiff prison and the Appeal Court set a date for 21 August. Shortly before his fate was to be decided, Grossley received the news that his two year-old son, Anthony, was dead. After Lily's death the boy had been placed in the care of her family in Aberdare. As Wales basked in a mid-August heatwave, the outdoor swimming pool in Cwmaman was packed with bathers. When the pool began emptying in the early evening two children saw what they first thought was a doll under the water. Attempts were made to revive the child but it was too late.

A week later the Appeal Court sat to hear Grossley's lawyers make their case. The defendant was present. The appeal rested on the biased nature of Judge Singleton's handling of the trial, especially his summing up. The Judge had failed to remind the jury, as was normal in capital cases, that if they have a reasonable doubt in their minds they must find the defendant not guilty. In this particular case, the question was whether or not the shooting had been an accident. The jury did not have to be convinced of this fact, merely to have doubt it was not the case. Not only had the Judge failed to clarify this point of law to them, he had gone so far as to dismiss it when submitted by the defence counsel.

In summing up, Judge Singleton had chosen to read out Grossley's first statement to the jury but omitted to add that it had been made while the defendant was in a hysterical state and, more importantly, that he had made a subsequent statement which had been corroborated by Lily. In his summary of the evidence the Judge should not only have reminded the Jury of this fact but should also have pointed out that both second statements were made independently of each other.

Judges have an obligation to present a rounded summary of the evidence admissible to a jury. In Grossley's case it would only have been fair for the Judge to refer to his injuries, which caused him to suffer from bouts of depression, a crucial detail as he had claimed he was trying to kill himself when he pulled the trigger; a point Lily had also made in her second statement. On the night in question Grossley had been drinking, surely a critical factor in the case of an accident involving a gun, and one that a judge should be obliged to point out to a jury. To ensure a just verdict, Judge Singleton should have also pointed out the lack of motive, or malice. The evidence showed they were a devoted couple.

Pre-meditation is a compulsory factor in proving murder, yet the Judge did not draw attention to the distinct lack of evidence proving malice aforethought. In fact Grossley had shown the gun to the Atkinson family – surely not the action of a man planning to use the weapon later that night for murder? Grossley's lawyers continued their arguments. In addition to his failure to include a number of points that might have helped the defence, Judge Singleton compounded the injustice by effectively making a case for the prosecution. It was wholly inappropriate for the Judge, in his remarks to the jury, to raise the proposition that a person must have intended the natural consequences of his own acts. If this generalisation was accurate surely there could never be a legitimate accident in law?

The most damning claims against the Judge's handling of the trial were reserved for his closing comments to the jury. The Judge had finished by asking three questions, all made rhetorical by the absence of balance to their content. First, why did Grossley take Lily out late at night? This insinuated, without any evidence, that it was Grossley's intention to murder her. Secondly, why had he taken the revolver out at night, when it had been kept upstairs before? The Judge omitted to mention that the gun was brought down as a result of a request from the landlady's son. Finally, why did Grossley make a false statement? In asking this question, Judge Singleton was remiss in not reminding the jury that Grossley was hysterical, drunk, and had in any event retracted his claims in a second statement.

Grossley's lawyers were confident that they had made an overwhelming case, if not for the guilty verdict to be overturned, then at least for a retrial. Two weeks later it was the Home Office that responded in a letter sent via the Director of Public Prosecutions. It stated that the Secretary of State had considered the case and decided that there was not "sufficient ground to justify him advising His Majesty to interfere in the due course of law."

With his final hope of a Royal Pardon dashed, on the day before he was due to be executed Grossley wrote a final letter to his foster parents in America.

Dearest Mother and Dad

Just a few lines, that I will ever be able to send you my dear.

For tomorrow at nine o'clock a.m. I will be no more, every one has been kind to me, and the Catholic priest has spent much time with me, he was most kind like you or dad would have been to me, I have made a general confession of my life, I feel quite at ease in leaving for the great beyond.

Believe me mother and dad, I am not guilty of this crime, before earthly judge, Yes. But not before God, the supreme judge of us all.

I feel quite calm now I have received the last sacraments this afternoon, in the chapel I asked God in his great mercy to be compassionate to me.

I am happy to go mother and dad even though I would of like to of seen you once more, well we will meet on the other side, God Bless you both for all you have done for me always.

You know what my life has been on earth so I am glad to leave now may be I will find peace in the next world.

I am sending you all my personal effects, and you will receive all my money from the Canadian Government, Ottawa, Canada, if you don't receive it soon write and ask about it comes to $1,000 do what you wish with it.

I wrote to Marie told her all about it.

I can't say any more the hour is drawing near so in my little composition you will know how I feel, and have always felt towards you both I never wanted to hurt you any more.

Goodbye Darling.
Your ever loving Son
Howard xxx

Howard Grossley was hanged at Cardiff Prison on 5 September 1945 and buried in the prison cemetery. Much of his background remains a mystery. There is no information of how his back was so badly burnt and it is unclear why someone of low rank would not have been repatriated following such a serious injury. Most mysterious of all is why the Bombardier is listed at Brookwood Military Cemetery as killed in action in 1943. A document relating to Howard Grossley at the British Public Records Office remains closed until 2034.

22. A NEST OF GENERALS

Immediately after his capture, General von Rundstedt was taken to the Palace Hotel in Luxembourg. Before the war it had been one of the most exclusive resorts in Europe and the American press were quick to complain that it was used to house leading Nazis. Von Rundstedt was unhappy at being placed amongst non-military members of the Nazi Party, but was soon moved to a more basic detention centre and from there to England. The Polish authorities had already formally registered von Rundstedt as wanted for war crimes, but the British were determined to keep hold of what was now their prize catch. They had many questions for him and the General spent most of that summer at Wilton House, Buckinghamshire, the headquarters of the Combined Services Detailed Interrogation Centre. Von Rundstedt greatly appreciated that his son, although a lower ranking officer, had been allowed to remain with him during this initial period of captivity. In fact it was General Montgomery who gave personal permission for the concession, reflecting the respect in which the veteran soldier was held by both British and American armies.

Many of von Rundstedt's senior colleagues were also at Wilton House. While most of Hitler's pseudo-military hierarchy had committed suicide, or fled for cover, the mainstream Army commanders had by and large surrendered themselves, British and American captivity being far preferable to Russian. On 17 July, General Ernst Busch died of a heart attack while at the interrogation centre and von Rundstedt requested his fellow officer be buried with the appropriate military honours. Twenty German Generals, along with British officers, walked behind the hearse as it passed von Rundstedt, who raised his Marshal's baton to signal the whole party to present arms. There was a spirit of mutual military respect between the former opposing sides at Wilton House. When the Japanese surrender was announced von Rundstedt made a point of formally offering his congratulations to the senior British officer.

In October 1945 von Rundstedt was transferred to Grizedale Hall in the Lake District, the original officers' POW camp. Again his son was allowed to accompany him. Here the General was visited several times by the respected military historian Sir Basil Liddell Hart and the two men would become close friends. By now von Rundstedt was suffering badly from arthritis, the condition probably aggravated by having to sleep on a standard issue POW bed. Much to the annoyance of the camp's commander, Liddell Hart arranged for a better mattress to be brought over from a local hospital. The historian was particularly interested in von Rundstedt's involvement in the two major plots to overthrow Hitler, in 1938 and 1944. He eventually concluded that although von Rundstedt was not directly involved with either plan, on both occasions the conspiring Generals looked to their figurehead to come forward as leader. Liddell Hart concluded that it was no real surprise when von Rundstedt failed to do so, not because he was afraid of the consequences but due to the fact that he was too upright a soldier to stage a coup. Von Rundstedt personally did not think the rank and file Army would ever revolt, though this conclusion may have been the result of his upbringing rather than an accurate indication of the strength of feeling at the time, certainly in 1944. General von Manstein, now also in British hands, best summed it up. "Prussian Field Marshals do not mutiny".

The Prisoner of War Interrogation Unit, still headed by Lieutenant Colonel Scotland, had metamorphosised into the War Crimes Investigation Unit. As the British and American press continued to print graphic photographs of liberated concentration camps, and amid competing claims from the governments of countries that had endured Nazi occupation, the Allies decided to hold a series of showcase war crime trials in Nuremberg. There were many obvious offenders to put into the dock but no decision had yet been made regarding the most senior ranks of the German Army, most of whom were captive in Britain, spread around various POW camps and interrogation units.

With no quick decision likely as to who would be charged, and with what crime, the Home Office placed all high-ranking German officers in one camp. The media had been critical of the high standard of comfortable imprisonment some of the German officers had enjoyed and Island Farm better fitted the stereotype image of a stark POW camp. None of the security defects, so apparent after the mass escape, had been rectified but it was considered unlikely that any of the Generals would attempt to tunnel under the dilapidated fences. The new Camp Commander, Grenadier Guardsman Major Denis Topham, was under strict instructions to treat his distinguished captives no differently from normal prisoners of war.

When it re-opened in November 1945, the renamed Special Camp

11 became a veritable 'Who's Who' of the German military elite. Von Rundstedt, who arrived on January 6 1946, was the most senior, and best known officer in the camp, but his rank of Field Marshall was shared by three others; Walther von Brauchitsch, Erich von Manstein and Ewald von Kleist.

Despite having von Brauchitsch in his pocket, Hitler had dismissed his Supreme Commander in December 1941, blaming him for the disasters in Russia. The Fuhrer assumed the role himself for the remainder of the war, while von Brauchitsch saw out the conflict in the comfort of his family estate, where he had surrendered to Allied troops. Von Rundstedt's protégé, von Manstein, the hero of the Ardennes campaign in 1940, had been rewarded with the command of Germany's 11th Army which he led as they occupied the Crimea. Transferred to northern Russia, von Manstein was responsible for the drawn out, and ultimately unsuccessful siege of Leningrad. Von Kleist had led the invasion of Yugoslavia in April 1941, before being given the thankless task of commanding Army Group A on the Eastern Front.

None of the two hundred officers housed at Island Farm were below the rank of General or its equivalent in the Kriegsmarine, Luftwaffe and Gestapo. They included Hermann Behrends, who had been in operational charge of VOMI, the elite S.S. security and intelligence service responsible for the elimination of enemies of the State; Werner Lorenz, Behrends' overall boss; Admiral Hans Voss, chief of warship construction and also Navy High Command, Norway; Hasso von Manteuffel, who although tasked with a supporting role, had made the deepest penetration of the Ardennes offensive; Gotthard Heinrici, a cousin of von Rundstedt who was Commander of the 4th Army until relieved of his post for ordering an Eastern Front retreat; Fridolin von Senger who had spearheaded the invasion of Holland and France and who, under Rommel in the 7th Panzer Division, took part in the capture of Le Havre and Cherbourg before leading the counter-offensive in Stalingrad and the defence of Monte Cassino in Italy; Gunther Blumentritt, von Rundstedt's Chief of Staff and latterly Commander of the 25th Army; Heinrich Ederbach, a veteran of Poland and the Eastern Front who briefly assumed command of the 7th Army in France; Hans von Ravenstein, a hero in Poland, France and Greece before taking a command in North Africa where he suffered the ignominy of becoming the first German General to be captured; Vice-Admiral Friedrich Huffmeier, overall Commander of the occupied Channel Islands; General der Waffen

S.S. Karl-Maria Demelhuber, who had the S.S. commands in Poland and France before becoming Commander of the S.S. in the Netherlands; Adolf Strauss, the Commander of the 9th Army; Heinrich-Gottfried von Vietinghoff, whose commands had included the 9th Army in Russia, the 15th Army in France and the 10th Army in Italy; Alexander von Falkenhausen, Military Commander of Belgium and Northern France but best remembered for his role in the 1944 assassination plot, captured while a prisoner in Dachau. Also in Camp 11 was the brilliant rocket scientist General Walter Dornberger, who throughout his captivity claimed his rank was a technicality and he should be treated as a civilian.

The Field Marshals, along with their batmen and basic staff, were given the comparative luxury of a complete hut to themselves. Von Rundstedt's son was still with him but suffering ill health himself by now. Shunning the S.S. officers, the traditional soldiers maintained a strict pecking order with von Rundstedt acknowledged as the senior officer. The official post of Camp Leader was given to Hans-Georg von Seidel, well qualified for an administrative role after serving most of the War as Quartermaster General of the Luftwaffe. Admiral Voss was made Camp Liaison Officer and with considerable media interest, and many column inches dedicated to speculating on the fate of the Generals, they appointed the English-speaking Fridolin von Senger as Press Officer.

A steady stream of senior British officers visited the camp, many having invented reasons to be there and merely taking the opportunity of meeting the more infamous of their former enemies face to face. Von Rundstedt was always a popular choice and the General was always courteous to his 'guests', in particular the Canadian Major Milton Shulman who, like Liddell Hart, was planning to write a book based on his findings.

Many of the prisoners at Island Farm had first hand experience of the major fronts and battles of the war, von Rundstedt more than most. He had also been responsible for making decisions – one in particular – that undoubtedly changed the course of the war. Von Rundstedt had overseen the implementation of *Blitzkrieg* and it was his backing of Manstein that had resulted in its use in the Ardennes offensive. Most military experts feel that the Western defences would have successfully stood up to Hitler's original invasion plan. It was von Rundstedt who had first given the order to halt the march into France, a decision – validated by Hitler – that allowed the British troops to retreat towards Dunkirk. Again, experts consider that if this evacuation had not taken place, Britain would not have fought on past 1940. A year later, had Hitler listened to von Rundstedt the decision to invade Russia would have been deferred until the following spring. He may then have succeeded. Had von Rundstedt's advice for an orderly retreat of the Eastern Front at the end of 1941 been heeded millions of lives would have been saved and the German Army would probably have retained the strength to overcome an Allied invasion. Von Rundstedt's method of defending the French coast, if he had been allowed by Hitler to properly implement it, may well have seen off the D-Day landings before vital footholds were gained.

Shulman was also fascinated to hear of von Rundstedt's relationship with Hitler. The General was disparaging about his former leader. "He didn't know the first thing about strategy – all he knew was bluff". Rundstedt's total lack of respect for Hitler was certainly not reciprocated. The elderly General laughed when he recalled how he was the only Army officer who was not forced to stand in the Fuhrer's presence: "Whenever I visited him, he always brought me a chair and made fat old Goering stand."

The problem facing the Allies was what to do with von Rundstedt and his fellow senior officers. The balance of public opinion clamoured for retribution. Fingering the surviving members of the Nazi Party in captivity and at large did not present a dilemma; that was provided by the assembled group of officers that were imprisoned in Island Farm. The Generals themselves were becoming increasingly worried, and frustrated, about their fate.

By the spring of 1946 the structure of the International Military Tribunal at Nuremberg had been decided. The four separate indictments were:

1: A common plan or conspiracy to seize power and establish a totalitarian regime.
2: Waging a war of aggression.
3: Violation of the laws of war.
4: Crimes against humanity, persecution and extermination.

Public relations dictated that priority should be given to putting the highest profile members of the Nazi Party on trial and twenty-two were immediately indicted. Not all had made it that far; the Norwegian Nazi leader, Vidkun Quisling, had already been shot by firing squad in Oslo.

The next priority, before individuals from the German armed forces could be tried for specific war crimes, was to ascertain the collective guilt of various organisations including the Reich Cabinet, S.S., S.A., Gestapo and the High Command and, most contentiously, the General Staff of the Wehrmacht. If the mainstream military was found guilty the implications were severe for the residents of Island Farm. When this news arrived, the officers decided that their collective honour should be defended at Nuremberg and the obvious man to do it was their Prussian doyen, von Rundstedt. In his formal notification to the trial von Rundstedt wrote that, at the request of his brother-officers, it was "the last task entrusted to my life to safeguard the honour of the German Army". On 15 May 1946 as von Rundstedt left Island Farm for Germany, 185 Generals and Admirals formed a guard of honour as he left the camp.

It was almost a month before he was called to the witness box. The questioning was tough but von Rundstedt stood his ground. He stated that neither he, nor his fellow officers were privy to the decisions to invade Poland, Norway, France, the Low Countries, the Balkans, Greece or Russia. Strategic matters were laid down by Hitler and not open to question. As field commanders they merely received orders to carry out these decisions. When asked why he had taken part in the invasion of Russia, if he personally opposed it, the General replied that he, and his colleagues, had sworn on oath, as a soldier, to do their duty.

When confronted with the issue of atrocities, von Rundstedt maintained that the Wehrmacht's code of honour meant that the laws of war were always strictly observed and offenders dealt with appropriately. In von Rundstedt's words, "severe measures were taken in the case of excesses, which in war can probably take place in all armies". When asked specifically about prisoners of war he stressed that there had been no intentional maltreatment – what had happened "at the rear" was not his responsibility. The General repeatedly made it clear to the court that he was not there to defend other organisations such as the S.S.

When the Prussian Code of Honour was raised von Rundstedt was adamant that senior soldiers of the German Army were "trained in the old soldierly traditions of decency and chivalry," adding "we endeavoured to hand them down to the younger officers." One prosecution lawyer, well prepared on military history, quoted the famous Prussian Field Marshal von Moltke to von Rundstedt, asking him if he agreed that an "officer bears a completely different responsibility in front of God and his Fatherland than merely the order of some superior?" Von Rundstedt, who at training college once paraded before the legendary officer, reacted angrily, reminding the questioner that he was not a cadet. When pressed for a reply the General chose his words carefully. "One is responsible for one's actions to God and one's Fatherland."

After two months von Rundstedt succeeded in his mission. The Wehrmacht was found not guilty on every count as an organised body. Forty years later, one of the British prosecuting lawyers, Peter Calvacoressi, recalled that von Rundstedt was never going to let on what he and his colleagues had known or done. "He did this well – or anyway successfully."

23. Closure

Although collective guilt was not to be attributed to the Werhmacht, each separate atrocity that had occurred during the war was investigated, and all senior German officers were to come under individual scrutiny. The British Government was divided as to how to handle the question of the German Generals after Nuremberg. There were members of the Cabinet who wanted to draw a line on the war as quickly as possible and move on with implementing sweeping social plans: on the other hand, the consensus of public opinion wanted visible justice. The situation was further complicated by the U.S., French, Polish and Russian Governments all pressing Britain to have individual Generals extradited for crimes alleged against their troops and citizens. When von Rundstedt arrived back at what he called 'Hotel Island Farm', the relief his colleagues had felt after the Nuremberg judgement was now outweighed by a general frustration that their period in captivity was obviously going to extend far beyond the end of the war.

The officers had now been joined by about a hundred and fifty lower ranking German prisoners. These men were housed separately and organised into daily groups dispatched to local farms; some were detailed to clean and cook for the officers. Across the country thousands of other Germans were being used on the many public works projects to repair war damage, prompting comment that this German labour was tantamount to slavery. Some of these prisoners, however, were perfectly content to remain in relative comfort. With their homes destroyed, and their families wiped out, there was little incentive to return to the desolation of post-war Germany.

At Island Farm there were separate issues for Major Topham to deal with in the autumn of 1946. Repatriation of German POWs had officially started in October 1946, but the British Government would not give any indication of the schedule for the release of senior officers in case subsequent allegations arose from the hundreds of investigations that were taking place from the Channel Islands to Stalingrad. The lower ranking prisoners had brought separate grievances to Major Topham. They were aware that prisoners in other camps enjoyed a much easier regime, to the extent that they were allowed unaccompanied trips outside of their camps. The prisoners at Island Farm felt they were being treated unfairly because of the presence of the officers, who, they also pointed out, were receiving more generous food rations. Some of the prisoners serving as orderlies to the Generals felt aggrieved that they were forced to be subservient to war criminals.

The key man in engineering a workable environment in the camp was Ted Lees, who had been appointed as camp interpreter when it re-opened and had built a relationship bordering on friendship with many of the Generals. Lees' real name was Erhard Wilhelm Saar. He had been born into a Jewish family living in the German city of Stettin (now Szczecin, Poland). His parents had divorced when he was a toddler and he went to live with his grandparents in Berlin. By 1934 the position for Jews was increasingly dangerous, but especially for the Saars as the boy's grandfather was an anti-Nazi activist in the Communist Party. Under the protection of Quakers, the thirteen-year old was smuggled to Britain. He would never see his German family again.

Adopting the name of his foster family, Lees left grammar school just as war broke out. After six weeks in an internment camp in Liverpool the British authorities were satisfied that he was not an 'enemy alien' and Lees was allowed to join the Pioneer Corps. Recognising his undoubted abilities and undercover potential as a natural German speaker, he was transferred into the Special Operations Executive. After extensive training, Captain Lees was parachuted into northern Italy to work with the local partisans on a variety of sabotage missions. When he left Italy at the end of the war he had acquired a local nickname, 'il Dynamitard'.

At Island Farm Lees convinced von Rundstedt, von Seidel and Voss of the merit of the prisoners taking part in an educational programme. He felt that the time at the Germans' disposal should be put to good use. In return for their full co-operation he would advocate a more relaxed regime. The Generals took part in daily classes, lectures and discussion groups that included English language tuition and an appreciation of the poetry of Byron. Tutors were a combination of British personnel and a panel of Germans including Anton von Bechtolsheim who had served as a Military Attaché in London and Washington before the war. Exams were set and certificates awarded. The British Government was keen to expose their captive audience to an extension of a wider de-Nazification programme to acclimatise the

Generals in preparation for an eventual return to civilian life in Germany and give them a greater appreciation of democracy. One particular lecture was entitled 'The British Way and Purpose'.

In October 1946 the authorities began individual screening aimed at repatriating those thought to be ready. The process would take several months but it had been decided that any General likely to be tried as a war criminal would have already been formally charged. As the S.S. had been found guilty as an organisation at Nuremberg, none of their personnel would be released. Field Marshall von Kleist was extradited that month to stand trial in Yugoslavia. He was eventually found guilty and sentenced to fifteen years imprisonment, from which he was extradited by the Russians, tried and given a life sentence. Von Kleist died in the Vladimir POW Camp on 16 October 1948.

The role of screening was given to a German, Otto John, who had worked during the war as a lawyer for Lufthansa, the national German airline. He was heavily involved in the 1944 bomb plot and used his Lufthansa connections to escape to Lisbon. He spent the remainder of the war working for a British-controlled German language radio station. John was particularly exercised by the question of why senior commanders – who must have realised Hitler was a criminal as early as The Night of the Long Knives in 1934 – continued to serve the Fuhrer. He saw his role at Island Farm as a unique opportunity to finally answer to this question.

Von Rundstedt was initially very resistant to John's intrusive methods but warmed after he made his son a priority for repatriation on health grounds. His own health was also in decline, most notably his increasing arthritis. Despite his lack of mobility he kept himself active with painting and collecting local fauna, which he carefully logged and pressed in a book. Major Topham realised there was no likelihood of his best-known prisoner making a run for freedom and the people of Bridgend became used to von Rundstedt, accompanied by his batman, walking around the local shops; the Corner Sandwich Bar in Wyndham Street being a particular favourite of the elderly officer. He also became a regular in the congregation of St Mary's Church, Nolton and was a much sought after guest at the more elite society soirées.

In August 1947, to the partial relief of the British Government, a medical board found von Rundstedt too ill to stand trial, and recommended repatriation. However in the same month Brigadier General Telford Taylor, the American Chief Counsel for War Crimes at Nuremberg, wrote to the British Attorney General saying he had a "very substantial amount of evidence" against all three Field Marshals at Island Farm. Taylor acknowledged that the Werhmacht had not been found guilty as a group but maintained that their leaders were a "ruthless military caste" who had been "responsible in large measure for the miseries and suffering that have fallen on millions of men, women and children". The Americans claimed they now had evidence that had not been available to the International Military Tribunal when von Rundstedt had appeared, which proved he had committed perjury.

The British Government was backed into a corner. With the exception of von Kleist, they had slowly been moving towards a decision to release the other three Field Marshals whose collective worsening health seemed to provide an ideal solution. Von Brauchitsch had been transferred from Island Farm to a military hospital in Stafford with a stomach complaint the previous April and von Manstein had been diagnosed with diabetes. The American bombshell could not be ignored but the British were not prepared to be pushed into a course of action with which they were becoming increasingly uncomfortable.

There were now fewer than ninety German Generals remaining at Island Farm, most having been given a clean bill of culpability by Otto John and subsequently repatriated. Public opinion was beginning to favour moving on and the Nuremberg clearance of the Werhmacht had, by and large, been accepted. It was becoming easier for people to simplify what had happened, blaming atrocities on the S.S. and Gestapo, not the main German Army.

Of the eleven S.S. officers at Special Camp 11, five would face charges. The Police Chief Lorenz was sentenced by a US military tribunal to twenty years imprisonment for his part in the crimes against humanity committed by his organisation VOMI. In his defence, Lorenz claimed that he was merely protecting German nationals in occupied countries, and in any event all the excesses were attributable to his deputy, Hermann Behrends. The British extradited Behrends to Yugoslavia, in February 1947, where a mass trial of S.S. officers was held. They were all found guilty, simultaneously executed by firing squad and buried in a mass, unmarked, grave.

The Waffen S.S. General Karl Wolf, who had surreptitiously tried to negotiate surrender to the Allies in Italy, gave evidence as a prosecution witness at Nuremberg. This appears to have helped his own case when it came to trial. He was sentenced by a German court to four years hard labour, but released after a week. Until 1961 he enjoyed a successful career in public relations until his comments in a magazine interview during the trial of the former S.S. officer Adolf Eichmann led to his being charged with having responsibility for the deportation of 300,000 Jews to the Treblinka concentration camp. He was found guilty and sentenced to fifteen years imprisonment.

Max Simon, another Waffen S.S. General, had already been tried in his absence by the Russians in 1943 for his part in the killing of 10,000 civilians in the town of Kharkov, and sentenced to death. The British refused post-war Soviet requests to return him to their care, choosing instead to try Simon before their own military tribunal, to be held in Italy where Simon had served in the latter part of the War. He was accused of complicity, in September 1944, of the massacre of up to 2,000 Italian civilians in reprisals for partisan activity. Found guilty, his death sentence was commuted, resulting in Simon serving seven years in a German prison. On his release he was re-arrested and charged with ordering the court martial and hanging of three German soldiers who had disarmed some Hitler Youth members to prevent them fighting American troops. Simon was twice acquitted of the charge on the grounds that he was following a legal order. He died shortly before the start of the third trial.

The other S.S. police officer being held at Island Farm was Generalleutnant Jakob Sporrenberg. One of the original S.A. stormtroopers, he had been a leader in the Hitler Youth movement during the 1930s and held wartime police chief commands in Russia, Poland and Norway. The British agreed to extradite him from Island Farm to Poland where he was eventually tried in 1950. Found guilty, he was hanged four years later.

The screening process at the camp took much longer than anticipated. A strong element of public opinion remained for the more notorious officers to be put on trial. The British Cabinet was also polarised, the treatment of three remaining Field Marshals, von Rundstedt, von Brauchitsch and von Manstein being the most fiercely debated issue.

While the political arguments continued, Island Farm received a new Commander. On his departure, von Rundstedt made a formal speech to Major Topham, thanking him, on behalf of his fellow officers, for the way that the Commander had fulfilled his difficult task. They appreciated Topham's "gentlemanlike chivalry" and how he always looked upon his charges "not as criminals and prisoners, but only officers in a really hopeless situation." Von Rundstedt concluded by presenting Topham with his treasured Field Marshal's baton.

When the incoming Commander, Major Charles Clements of the 4th Hussars, arrived in September 1947 he immediately made conditions even more tolerable for the high-ranking inmates. Having been a prisoner of war himself Clements felt that the War Office was too burdened by red tape and political opinion, resulting in the prisoners being treated far too severely. Von Rundstedt told the new commander that apart from the length of time being taken to decide about repatriation, there was one major day-to-day grievance he might be able to resolve. In return for an assurance that they would behave like gentlemen, Clements agreed that all the German officers would now be allowed out of the camp without accompaniment by a guard. He went so far as removing live ammunition from the camp guards, the majority of whom he rated no higher than his predecessor, Commander Darling. The locals in Bridgend quickly became used to having uniformed German Generals in their midst. Many lasting friendships were made.

Clements became friendly with von Rundstedt over the next few months, frequently visiting his quarters for tea. The British Commander would discreetly leave a packet of quality cigarettes for von Rundstedt, a chain-smoker, knowing that the German found the canteen supply to be of a very inferior quality. When von Rundstedt received news, just before Christmas, that his son was seriously ill, Clements pulled the necessary strings for the old officer to be given compassionate leave to return briefly to Germany. Being reunited with his wife after almost two and a half years was traumatic for von Rundstedt. Bila was practically destitute, as all of the family's money had been held in what was now the Russian sector of Germany. Two weeks after von Rundstedt returned to Island Farm his son died.

Although the British had still not made any decision on what to do with the Field Marshals, procedures were now well under way to charge five of the non-S.S. Generals at Island Farm. General Kurt Student of the Luftwaffe was tried before a British military court in Germany accused of war crimes committed by troops under his command in Crete. He was found guilty on three of the eight charges, all relating to the abuse and killing of Allied prisoners of war. Sentenced to five years imprisonment, Student was released after serving two, as the trial verdict had not been properly confirmed.

General Franz Bohme was placed on trial before a U.S. military tribunal in Nuremberg, charged with various humanitarian crimes in

Serbia. He chose to jump to his death from the 4th floor of his local prison prior to the case being heard. A British court in Italy found General Eduard Crasemann guilty of involvement in the mass execution of 175 civilians near Florence in August 1944. He died after three years of a ten year prison sentence. Karl von Beeren was found not guilty by the British of playing a part in the execution of twenty Royal Engineer commandos caught attempting to destroy a heavy water plant in Norway. The most senior of the group, General Adolf Strauss, was charged with various crimes against civilians and Allied POWs but his trial never took place as he was released on health grounds.

Soon after returning from Germany, von Rundstedt underwent another series of medical tests. Both von Manstein and von Brauchitsch were, by now, hospitalised in the north of England. The British still maintained that none of the Field Marshals were fit to stand trial, and were beginning to form the view that the preparation of charges was too complicated. The Americans persisted, especially in the case of von Rundstedt. Feelings in the U.S. were still running high after full details of the massacre of American soldiers at Malmedy became public. The Belgian Government, however, had concluded that von Rundstedt was not as guilty as first thought and had no objection to his release. France maintained that, as Commander-in-Chief in the West, von Rundstedt must at least be partly responsible for atrocities that occurred during his command. The Soviets were also requesting his extradition.

Von Rundstedt's health deteriorated to the point where he needed to be hospitalised. In May 1948, with plans in place to close Camp 11, notice was received that von Rundstedt was to be transferred to a military hospital in East Anglia. Commander Clements and his officers held a dinner in the General's honour and invited Major Topham back for the occasion. Before he left Island Farm for the last time Rundstedt presented a silver crucifix to St Mary's Church and wrote to the Bishop of Llandaff praising the local rector, Dean Gravell. The General's familiar walking sticks were given to friends in Bridgend as mementos of his stay in the town. The veteran German officer had become part of the local community and was known affectionately behind his back as 'Papa Rundstedt'.

Three months later American policy prevailed and all three Field Marshals were charged with a succession of war crimes. The cases would be heard at a specially convened British court in Hamburg and the three elderly men were to be held in a prison hospital in the city while the lengthy legal preparations ground on. By now, relations between von Rundstedt and von Manstein had become very strained.

Feldmarschall von Brauchitsch died of a heart attack on 18 October, soon after they had arrived in Hamburg. Seven months later there was still no immediate prospect of the trials commencing. Russia was pressing for the extradition of both von Rundstedt and von Manstein, quoting a recent United Nations ruling that war criminals should be returned to the scene of their alleged crimes for trial. The British argued that as von Rundstedt was charged with twenty crimes, spread across Russia, Poland, Holland, Belgium and France it was not reasonable, or practical, to try him in every jurisdiction.

Meanwhile, in Britain, Basil Liddell Hart had begun a media campaign and co-ordinated a powerful political lobby to have von Rundstedt released. By May 1949 the historian's efforts had built up a head of steam, with the Bishop of Chichester moving a motion in the House of Lords that all war crime trials be halted immediately and a general amnesty granted. At the last minute the Lord Chancellor intervened and recommended that von Rundstedt be released on medical grounds.

Von Manstein, now the only German General facing British charges, eventually stood trial on seventeen counts in August 1949. He was found guilty of nine offences and sentenced to eighteen years imprisonment, later reduced to twelve on appeal. The fact that he had been found guilty was not lost on those that had been pressing for Rundstedt to face similar charges.

The remainder of von Rundstedt's life was spent in discomfort and poverty. He lived with his wife in a spartan two room Red Cross apartment just north of Hamburg until 1950 when Liddell Hart brokered a deal with 20th Century Fox to allow von Rundstedt's portrayal in the film *Rommel – Desert Fox*. The actor Frederic Marsh played the part of von Rundstedt; Liddell Hart, writing to his friend, ensured him that the characterisation would be "dignified and sympathetic". In the same year von Rundstedt's faithful Chief of Staff, Gunther Blumentritt was commissioned by a British publisher to write a biography of his former boss and immediately gave half of the advance to his subject. These two windfalls allowed the von Rundstedts to move into the relative comfort of a three room flat above a shoe shop in Hamburg. Bila died in October 1952. Four months later von Rundstedt passed away of heart failure.

Obituaries were varied. The *Daily Mail* called him "the Grand

Old Man of the German Army". The *Guardian* saw his life as "an essay in Prussian orthodoxy". The *Telegraph* felt "he had the virtues and failings of the typical Prussian aristocrat". The *Daily Sketch's* headline simply read "Prisoner-of-War No 816209 is dead"; adding underneath "a martinet who believes a soldier has only one duty – OBEY [sic]". Von Rundstedt's last public statement was an introduction to an American magazine article written by Blumentritt. In it he wrote "Nothing can be beautiful or is excused. Unfortunately, all of us make mistakes."

Shortly after von Rundstedt left Island Farm the remaining 81 officers and 153 men were released. Many of the lower ranks chose to stay in south Wales and married local women. The most unusual route to freedom was that of the V-Rocket scientist Walter Dornberger, whose refusal to be associated with the German military had made him highly unpopular in Special Camp 11. Along with Werner von Braun, his boss at Peenemunde, he was headhunted by the Americans to spearhead their embryonic space programme. Dornberger had uttered some of the most visionary words of the war when he proclaimed, "we have invaded space for the first time; we have proved rocket propulsion practical for space travel. This third day of October 1942, is the first of a new era of transportation, that of space travel."

In many respects a small patch of land in south Wales had been a microcosm of many aspects of the war. The complex of small, austere, rooms had provided temporary homes to Welsh munitions workers, being subjected to German bombing, and German soldiers plotting their escape home to a country being systematically destroyed. The same concrete walls had been stared at both by American G.I.s contemplating their forthcoming fate on the beaches of France, and the most senior German officer wondering if he was to be made accountable for the actions of a million men who had served under him. Many paths crossed during World War Two and perhaps it was fitting that when he died, as a mark of military respect, the American 29th Infantry Division buried one of von Rundstedt's shoulder straps at their headquarters underneath a stone that they had brought home from Normandy.

EPILOGUE

Four of the Generals who were repatriated from Island Farm were subsequently brought to trial. In March 1951, Alexander von Falkenhausen was sentenced in Brussels to twelve years imprisonment for his role in the deportation of approximately 25,000 Belgium Jews, and for the execution of hostages. He was released three weeks later. Hermann-Bernhard Ramke, a Luftwaffe General, was found guilty of war crimes by a French court in 1951. He received a sentence of five years hard labour but was pardoned two months later. Hasso von Manteuffel, the Panzer General who had been in command at the Battle of the Bulge, appeared in 1959 before a West German court and was found guilty of ordering one of his men to be shot for negligence while commanding in Russia in January 1944. He was sentenced to eighteen months in prison but released after eight weeks following the intervention of the West German President. In 1953, Georg Benthack was tried in Hamburg on manslaughter charges. He was accused that in the last weeks of the war he had ordered the execution of four men under his command, without giving them the benefit of a court martial. The German jury acquitted him, arguing that he was following the orders of his High Command, which had given senior officers the authority to maintain discipline as they saw fit. Benthack stated to the court, "I would do it again".

After the last prisoner had left, Island Farm remained unused for over forty years, its buildings slowly falling into disrepair. In 1993 the Council decided to demolish the huts, prompting protest from local people. Although the camp was eventually flattened, Hut 9, with its tunnel still intact, was given listed building status and repaired. As the other huts were demolished, the artwork on their walls was carefully removed and put into storage.

In 2002 Island Farm became the subject of a massively contentious, and ultimately unsuccessful, planning application to build a hotel, houses and a sports complex for the Welsh Rugby Union on the site. The Island Farm Heritage Association has now been formed and plans to convert Hut 9 into a museum.

Acknowledgements

This book would not have been possible without the assistance of Brett Exton who runs an excellent and much visited website about the camp: http://www.islandfarm.fsnet.co.uk

In addition, my grateful thanks go to the staff at Coed Parc Library, Bridgend; Cardiff Reference Library; Glamorgan Records Office; The Public Records Office; Collindale Newspaper Library; and The Eisenhower Library, Abilene KS. I am also indebted to Andrew Evans, Joe Ludlow, Bridgend Civic Trust, Steve Jebson, the National Meteorological Office, Steve Maitland-Thomas, Albert J. Yascavage, William O. Hickok and the 28th Infantry Division Association, Andrew E. Woods, First Division Museum, Cantigny Il, Sonny Atkinson, Joan and Frank Knights, Rob Davis, Herb Pankratz, Phyllis Blue, Greg J. McCooeye, National Archives of Canada, Fiona Darling.

Index

Related Titles

F.S.P. – Arthur Gwynn-Browne

The story of the terrible retreat to and triumphant evacuation from Dunkirk of the British Expeditionary Force. Absorbing, affecting, thrilling, often funny, this book was the first on-the-ground account of Dunkirk to be published (in 1942), and lacks nothing in its immediacy.

F.S.P. is revolutionary in the author's immersing of the reader in the psychological turbulence of the retreating soldiers. This is not only a gripping narrative but also one into which the reader is drawn and, like the participants, debilitated. The peculiarity, the optimism, apprehension, raw fear and bitter sense of defeat of the soldiers are transferred to the reader by a modernist style through which the reader also feels the stress of having lived in 'a continuous present' of four days without sleep. The result is a stunningly authentic and involving record of the experience of Dunkirk.

£7.99 paperback

Kerry's Children – Ellen Davis

Ellen Davis was born in 1929 in rural Germany. Her Jewish family had lived in the same village since 1760 but its peaceful existence was shattered when Hitler came to power. This autobiography tells the harrowing story of her childhood struggle to protect her younger brothers and sisters from Nazi persecution until her escape to Britain via the Kindertransport.

Against the background of her life in a new country, Ellen continues to search for her German family and relatives, in Australia, Israel and the US – a search which ends, heart-rendingly, in Riga in Latvia.

£7.99 paperback

Collected Poems – Alun Lewis

A reluctant volunteer because of his pacifist leanings, Alun Lewis became perhaps the leading writer of the Second World War. His poems and stories about life as a soldier were both popular and critically acclaimed. He died on active service in Burma, aged 28. This *Collected Poems* includes all of his two published collections, plus some 27 previously uncollected and published poems.

£9.99 paperback

A Stranger at Home – Denis F. Ratcliffe

A gripping and exhaustively researched novel of conflicting ideologies in Central Europe. During the Thirties Favel Steiger is caught up in the passion and betrayal of Czech politics. A gifted young man, he is sent to the Soviet Union for training, where he becomes a member of the Communist Party. Arriving back in Czechoslovakia in 1938 he is caught in the German occupation of the Sudetenland and joins the S.S. It is perhaps inevitable that his unit becomes part of the 6th Army Group which is trapped at Stalingrad. Can Favel translate himself from S.S. officer to Soviet Communist Party member as the battle lines ebb and flow?

A Stranger at Home is a panoramic novel stretching from a childhood in England to the degradations visited upon the populations of middle Europe as the war grinds bitterly and brutally to its conclusion. As a record of what fate can deal out it is not to be missed.
£7.99 paperback

Love & War – Siân James

Siân James brings her customary narrative flair and ear for dialogue to this beautifully-observed novel of love, scandal and grief set in wartime rural Wales. For three years, a young teacher has patiently awaited the return of her soldier-husband, but her loneliness and her feelings for a past lover pitch her into a conflict of loyalties and duty. Perceptive, funny and moving, *Love & War* is a poignant and beautifully-plotted portrait of the Home Front.
£6.99 paperback

Crystal Spirit – Roger Granelli

Denied his freedom through marriage and work a young man embraces the Labour Movement, and volunteers for the International Brigade in the Spanish Civil War. This is a gripping and affecting novel, persuasive and realistic, sympathetic in its portrayal of life in the Depression and full of remarkable scenes from the Spanish Civil War. Closely researched, *Crystal Spirit* brings to life a period which has almost slipped from memory. It is a moving testament to those who suffered in Wales and Spain, yet remained undefeated by the horrors of poverty and a brutal war.
£7.99 paperback